D1825751

COUNTRYMAN'S MEMOIRS

Ted Eales

COUNTRYMAN'S MEMOIRS

A Warden's Life
on
Blakeney
Point

© W. E. R. Eales, B.E.M. 1986

Published for W. E. R. Eales, B.E.M., by Jim Baldwin
Publishing, Fakenham.
Distributed to the trade by Paper Klip
(Wholesale), Fakenham, Norfolk.

ISBN 0 948899 00 X

Edited by
SHEILA WYER

Typeset by Fakenham Photosetting Ltd.
Originated by Colourplan, Printed by
Colour Print and bound by Dickens Print
Trade Finishers.

A Product of Fakenham

Acknowledgements

When writing a book of this nature, one has to seek help from time to time and I am pleased to say that all those approached were very generous in this respect.

Anglia Television have been a great support to me as have two of my friends connected with this company, Dick Joice and Vic Birtles.

Others have given or loaned me photographs or perhaps jogged or refreshed my memory. Thanks to Mrs. P. Catling, Mrs. P. Oliver, Mrs. J. D. Lewis, Mr. S. Webster, Mrs. Digby, Mrs. A. Athill and Mr. A. J. Sampson for allowing me to use his map.

On the production side I must thank Sheila Wyer for her editing and Jill Perrywarnes and Marylin Wyer for the typing.

Above all my thanks to all who visited and enjoyed Blakeney Point and made my life there so worthwhile and satisfying.

Ted Eales

Foreword

By Lord Buxton

Nothing could give me greater pleasure than to introduce this engaging story, the life and times of Ted Eales of Blakeney Point. Every reader will find it a privilege to become immersed in its pages, because it is much more than just a good bit of reading. It is like sitting down for an hour or two and listening to Ted talking about his life in his incomparable manner, so widely known and enjoyed by his television audiences and by the tens of thousands of visitors to the Point, especially school parties, when he was warden.

In these rather disturbing times in which we live, everyone will gain a sense of reassurance that there are still people who have such a complete feeling of contentment and satisfaction with all that they have experienced. Ted loves the Point and the Saltings, he loves his friends and neighbours in the villages, he loves the visitors, and the creeks and the boats, the birds and the fish, and all other forms of wildlife. In fact he loves everything, a man fulfilled and at peace with his existence.

Ted Eales has been one of my best friends for over half a century. My first memory of him was when, at the age of sixteen, I was sleeping on a house boat in Blakeney harbour. At about five in the morning a young fellow with an impish grin knocked me up and asked if I would like to catch dabs in the creek. We have been close companions ever since.

Ted speaks warmly of all his friends and neighbours in the area, and particularly of the famous families in Morston, Blakeney and Cley. It is intriguing to hear of the close collaboration with his old friend and colleague Billy Bishop, the warden of Cley marshes, and of how they operated a sort of partnership between these two notable wildlife reserves.

This book is a must for every lover of North Norfolk and for every naturalist and bird watcher. I am grateful to Ted for allowing me to pay my own tribute.

Stiffkey
Norfolk   Aubrey Buxton

1 | Before the War, the Founding of the Nature Reserve

Many of my friends, far and wide, as soon as they heard that I was retiring from Blakeney Point in 1980 said, "Oh you must write a book, Ted – you must have plenty to tell us – what about it?" This went on for several years after I had retired. Unfortunately I had an illness which held me back from any activity. Nevertheless I had time to think, and look at old photographs and various bits of news from the past. It is very difficult to start, especially being the first time I have ever tried anything like this, but here it is. The best and I suppose the most interesting years of my life have been the fifty-one or two years I spent on Blakeney Point. The War years of course were a bit more exciting at times but we start first of all with Blakeney Point.

My parents took on the job in 1928–29. The first year they were appointed in charge of the Tea and Refreshment Room. My father was to have a year with the original Warden Bob Pinchen, to get used to the routine and the handling of people, and the learning of all the bits and pieces of Wardening. I was about eleven years old or less, and actually I was on the pay roll from the word go, because I was appointed "Litter Collector" by Professor Oliver. He was the man who taught me everything I was to know about Blakeney and its life, birds, vegetation, people and how to handle them. I was getting, at that particular time, sixpence a week in war savings stamps. They were stuck on a card every week. I collected litter and assisted my father with many of his duties.

In the early days Professor Oliver looked into the problem of controlling visitors so as not to disturb the wildlife unduly. He allowed for an average of between sixty and a hundred local families. They could enjoy the atmosphere of the sand dunes and foreshore, and the men could sail or fish or collect cockles. This helped to subsidise their low weekly earnings. From mid April to mid October on what was known as Point Sunday (morning and evening tides) an armada of every type of craft would descend on the Point. They would unload their cargo of families, pets, primus stoves, and primitive cooking utensils. The men, with their sons, could be seen frantically digging lugworms on the ebb tide. Within half an hour enough bait was dug to provide a two-hour flat fish session in the Pit and down the Narrows, to the very last worm if the fishing that day was good.

At lunchtime the weary fishermen could be seen seeking their families in the dunes. The womenfolk would prepare a meal, often a plate of hot cockles gathered and cooked in salt water during the morning. The more wealthy of these parties would bring a flagon of beer and perhaps a cold chicken. Evidence from litter after they had gone would show the odd Tern's egg had been eaten for dessert. On the flood tide, fishermen could be seen hard at it, in tight formation, hauling in three or four flatfish at a time. Their total bag on a good Sunday could be between a hundred and a hundred and twenty. At sunset a stream of people would be seen to leave the dunes and converge on the beaches and sandflats around Pinchens Creek, to be picked up and taken back to their respective quays and creeks. Such was the use of this unique reserve in pre-war days.

At the end of the day I, as a teenager, could be seen collecting a few sackfulls of litter. This would be of varied description, and would be burned or buried by my father. The more litter, the better the day the children of Blakeney would have had.

The visitors in those days who came with an interest in natural history were mainly local aristocracy, members of the Norfolk Naturalists, Landowners, etc. as well as a small number of what we now call "weekend parishioners" who owned their own boats and employed their own boatmen the year round.

So the Point Sundays came and went and I learned more and more with my parents – my father was Warden by that time. I thoroughly enjoyed it, as I loved sailing. Sailing was my main love and as soon as I could afford it and my parents could afford it, they bought me an old boat for about five quid. The next thing I knew, a chap, a very good friend of everybody, sat and watched me with my bits of rag up, as an apology for sails, and old bits of sheet and he said, "Ted it is time you had a proper sail – I will buy you one" and he bought me what I thought was a magnificent lug-sail of about fifty-five square feet. I thought I was the "King Pin" with my new mast and I used to spend many hours sailing, mainly back to the village to get the bread and milk every morning, as the tide was suitable, or to fetch my grandmother over for the day from the village.

The only sad thing about my early days was that I had to go to school, and I had to lodge during the week in the village with my grandparents while I attended Blakeney School with two or three other boys from Morston Village. I had to come back reluctantly on a Sunday night to start the week's school on the Monday morning. I tried having a headache, or sore throat, but my father got used to that dodge and I was taken ashore to my grandparents whether I was, as I thought, half dead or not. That was my life in the early days.

Many jobs I had to do with my father because in those days the Terns were just as numerous, in fact more numerous I think, Common Terns in particular. There was no proper control with regards to fencing off – this I introduced later on, when I became Warden. In those days I had to chop a lot of sticks about two feet long, so that we could stick, as we used to call it, every nest. We put a stick about two feet from the nest to warn people where the eggs were, on shingle and sand. People were conducted around the Terneries in little groups. This was the worst thing you could do to a nesting colony of Terns. There was a constant flow of visitors going round, certainly during the incubation period, although these Terns got used to it. They nested in and amongst the shingle and the heat from the stones was like a hot water bottle. I realised that very few of the eggs came to any harm, except if you had bad weather or a storm or two.

The Common Tern was our main headache. My mother very often used to brag and say "They will not nest until my Birthday" which was the 13th May, and sure enough within two or three days of her birthday the first Common Tern eggs would be found. Lesser Terns were more precious of course and still are. The Sandwich Tern fluctuated, some years you would have a hundred, another four hundred and another year none at all, and that is how it went on. In those days we had a charming member of the Tern family, one or two Roseate Terns which were a treasure and to be guarded closely from the egg collectors. Lots of stories can be told about egg collecting.

Nevertheless as the years drifted on I left school (to my delight). I should have gone to Grammar School, but I dodged that one and said that I would rather stop on Blakeney Point and continue learning the natural way, because Professor Oliver spent many months on the Point. He was the Founder Member for the National Trust in the original days. In 1912 he handled the conveyance and the gift of Blakeney Point for the people of Blakeney and district and gave the Point to the Trust and he also negotiated the sale of odd bits and pieces on behalf of the National Trust. So he was, to my mind, the National Trust, and everybody loved him and everybody co-operated with him, the fishermen in particular. There are lovely stories about him in his early days and when the Lifeboat House was being converted in 1921–22–23 I think it was, Professor Oliver managed to persuade the Lifeboat Institution to give the building to the National Trust for a Warden's House. The original lifeboat house, known as the Black Hut, then became a University Hut. London University still hold the lease. It is a lovely traditional old hut. Both these buildings were converted into living

11

accommodation under the supervision of the professor. Walter Allen was the chief carpenter, helped by two apprentices, Kenny Newton and his brother.

Professor Oliver stayed on the Point with these workmen. He was there to oversee their work and keep them supplied. As far as I can see he almost fed them. Only the other day I was talking to Kenny and I said, "Do you remember the Christmas you spent on Blakeney Point with Professor Oliver? I will always remember it," he said, "the old man was so generous and kind." He used to walk and get the stores and at this particular Christmas we were all there trying to get the job finished and we decided to stop there over the holiday. He went off to Cley and didn't say a word of what he was going to do. The next thing we knew he was carrying a small Christmas tree, parcels, and a bag full of chickens, sausages, fruit and drinks. On Christmas Day he had this tree decorated in the Lifeboat House with a present for all of us workmen tied to each branch – what a gesture. I wonder how many people would do that today. Not many of them he said, "Too b . . . . y far for them to walk now!" That was just one very nice story from the past of that character who still lives today, God bless him, a dear old friend of many people. Kenny learnt the hard way like many of us.

As time went on the huts on Blakeney Point were occupied from Easter until the end of September at least. When I grew old enough I was their Postman, come Baker, come Milkman and I had to go ashore every day and get my mother's supplies of milk and bread for the Tea Room, her letters and the *Eastern Daily Press*. I had a lovely old labrador who would often go ahead of me with the *E.D.P.* in his mouth and deliver it to my father, post-haste, so to speak, about 8 o'clock in the morning. I would come lingering behind with the 24 pints of milk, and umpteen loaves of bread. That was my life on Blakeney Point.

During the day if there was nothing much to do, I would go down to the low water mark and watch the fishermen and learn from them and do a bit of "butt pricking" if you know what that is. "Butts" were the fish, sometimes called flounders, and if you were shown properly and learnt the right way you could make your own little spear. They used to make these "Butt Forks" as they called them with barbs on them. The Blacksmith used to make them, but I preferred an ordinary steel skewer, or something similar on the end of a nice light piece of bamboo. I could slowly walk about the place with bare feet with water just below the knees, or higher up still if the water was clear, and very often fill a side bag full of these flat fish by spearing them. Marvellous sport and very tricky to learn, until you knew the habits of these old fish and where to look for them. It was good fun. That was one of my very many pastimes, and I learnt the tricks of the trade from several fishermen with regards to sailing, fishing and anything you could mention in their line, even worm digging. At that time mussel fishing was a big industry in Blakeney

Harbour. It has died out a bit now because the mussel beds have not been kept up, the harbour has silted up and the mussel beds are not as good as they could be. One or two youngsters still carry on with the mussels I think, but in those days, local people had to get their living from the estuary and around it in all kinds of ways. Collecting samphire, cockles, lugworms, mussels or butts.

You could catch sea trout at night along the beaches in the right weather. What a marvellous pastime or sport that was and a living for the fishermen. They would use long nets and a dinghy, if they could get out there, but we "walked in" as we called it. We had a twenty-five-yard net, with the right mesh for mackerel, because that was about the right size for catching the old trout. The best time was at low tide, just as it began to flood. One of us would walk in as deep as we could, the other chap would stay on the beach or go just in to the edge of the breakers, until the net was in a bow shape. The chap out deep was well ahead of the other fellow, so as soon as he saw a fish strike the net he would come in quickly to trap it. Now sea trout came ashore not to feed but to use the waves to rub the sea lice off their backs. They, like many fish, had lots of sea lice and this was a method of removing them. They could roll to and fro in the breakers, hence we could catch many of them while they were de-licing. Sometimes we worked all night and caught nothing. On the other hand sometimes we caught a huge trout. The biggest trout, or two, that I ever caught was when I was fishing with Billy Bishop the Warden at Cley Marshes. He and I used to get together and do a bit of trouting, drawing the shore, and on this occasion Billy and I clicked. We had two of the biggest specimens that I had ever seen. One was fourteen-and-a-half and the other nearly fourteen pounds and we have got a picture of them which we are delighted to boast about, as the other fishermen had said that we would not get more than five or six pounds. You could always get three-and-six a pound or three bob a pound or half a crown in those days from the local hotels. That was a good night's work for us when we were lucky.

The flat fish on the seaward side were much nicer to eat than those in the harbour that lived in the estuary and fed on lugworm. The flat fish on the beach itself were mainly called "Sandling", small plaice, there were also lots of turbot about the size of a large dessert plate or dinner plate and these were delicious fish. Now and again if you were lucky you could get round a few mackerel when they came inshore after the whitebait, which is the main food for the mackerel. You could nip round a few of them right quickly, but you had to be damn quick! Then there was the Mullet. The Gray Mullet was very clever, he could jump the net like a greyhound, straight out of the sea over the top of the net, if you weren't crafty enough to hold your net in the right position. I could go on about fishing for the next three days I reckon, but I think we had better draw on to other experiences.

13

My life started to develop because by the time I was sixteen I was relied upon for all sorts of little jobs by my parents. I used to paint the old Lifeboat House with my father. He loved that job because that was the old naval colours, dark admiralty grey on the roof and light admiralty grey on the sides. We used fifteen gallons of a special metal paint, as it was corrugated iron. My father was delighted to get on top of that roof with his long-handled brush and have me on a ladder on the sides, and it took us about a week to paint the place if we had the weather we needed. On one occasion, and I always tell my relations this story, we were painting away and my father was on his knees painting down towards me near the troughing on the curb. I was just below him on the ladder, and I said something to annoy him. He started shouting at me and his top teeth flew out, slid over the nice wet grey paint and lodged in the gutter. Luckily for me, as if not, I should never have been forgiven. Anyway I salvaged these top teeth and we gave them a wash off with petrol to get the paint off and then all was well.

But you don't forget those little incidences and I could not have had a better parent than him. Being ex-navy you nearly stood to attention for him at times and the day the local agent or chairman of the committee came over we had to whitewash the steps, and every stone was polished within the vicinity of ten yards of the doorstep! A typical naval tradition for an admiral's inspection. This was laughed about many times by the local fishermen who respected my father and pulled his leg about his naval traditions. Sadly in 1939 he became ill and died suddenly, and that particular year I was appointed Warden in his footsteps. My father died in March 1939 and in April I found myself, at twenty years old, Warden of Blakeney Point.

My mother was a standby as well as various relations in the village. I felt much responsibility was placed on me because although I knew every inch of the job and what happened there, we had all sorts of worries with not just Wardening Blakeney Point but you had to worry about the people who took risks sailing in and out of the harbour and swimming. All sorts of sad occurrences could happen and *did* happen right through the years I was on Blakeney. Nevertheless things went fairly well. I was roped in to Chamberlain's Militia because the war was about to start and I also registered through that scheme on the Royal Navy Special Reserve, and I was delighted to be able to get into the navy to follow my father's footsteps. In spite of the fact that I was born with a little bit of "ticker trouble" (I had a leaky valve) they told me that I would never get into the navy or army. But hold you on boy I did, didn't I? I tricked the old doctors in Norwich when we went up for our examinations and I was fairly fit because I could keep up with anybody else. Blakeney Point I had to thank for that fitness in my early days. The war came along which was another period of excitement and drama.

Like many other chaps with me there is much to be told and so I will continue this when I get in the mood and can think of all the various incidences which I can relate without too much drama.

Having found myself appointed Warden at the early age of twenty I very often thought to myself how quickly the time had passed, because I think about how I was introduced to the Point by my parents and fishermen and all the other people who helped me to realise what a life it was. In particular, the winter months were very interesting as well as summer, because as soon as I had left school, and even before then, I used to help my uncle to kill the rabbits, a job which my father passed on to him, because technically speaking the rabbits on Blakeney Point had to be kept down very severely and they were part of the Warden's duties and wages in those days. The Wardens were very poorly paid and my father was lucky in a way, I suppose, he was a naval pensioner which meant that he had a little bit more than the usual income for a Warden and he could afford to let my uncle help him kill the rabbits and share the revenue which later I took on as well. They had to be trapped, because amongst the sand dunes it was very difficult to catch rabbits. One might think that it would be easy but it was not, because they burrowed into the sand and if you used a ferret they would scrap ahead of the ferret and tuck up, as we called it. You can't dig them out, the sand dunes are too deep. You could dig them in in odd places in a shallow area, but not very often. So we had to use gin-traps which are banned today and we used to run about a hundred and twenty traps starting from the Hood which was the farthest point East. There were many rabbits on the old Hood hills which formed the original Point of that peninsula. We used to get as many as twenty – thirty if we were lucky on the first day and then they would leave the trap set for three days in the same places and would take out those rabbits that had been caught each morning.

We were very lucky because the butchers on the mainland took the rabbits for food, they were the main diet of the country people. Our rabbits at Blakeney for some unknown reason produced a lot of fat and they were good heavy rabbits, feeding on the marshes and the areas which went down to the mud flats and hence the butchers clamoured for them and we got about twopence more a head than for the land rabbits. That is to say that if we were lucky we could get a shilling a rabbit whereas the farmers on the mainland only got tenpence a rabbit for theirs and so if ever they heard that they were Point rabbits they were worth another twopence more. We were delighted, twopence to us was a lot of money in those days and hence the winters came and went and I gradually learnt the trade of vermin killing. Amongst rabbits of course there are lots of rats and the odd stoat. The rats were a menace to the nesting population of the Terns, and the stoat was even worse. Which you will probably realise when you see from the illustrations the damage a

15

stoat could do. When an old bitch stoat has young, then she has to kill dozens of birds and chicks every night!

Wildfowling was another main sport of Blakeney Harbour for generations. Since my grandfather was at one time Head Keeper on Sir Alfred Jodrell's estate at Bayfield Hall (where my mother was born), I had it in my blood I suppose to carry a gun and shoot rabbits and wildfowl, and many of the fishermen got their living by wildfowling in the winter months. Punt gunning for Wigeon and other wild duck was a common thing which is really a long episode if I were to go into detail. I used to flight the Wigeon in certain areas, because they flighted onto feeding grounds around the estuary, the "Wigeon Grass" as we used to call it, which they fed on (Eel Grass if you like). They also fed on the samphire beds which seeded in the winter months. The Teal especially loved the samphire seeds.

The wildfowling still goes on under a stricter routine, the Wildfowl Association of Blakeney and District control the shooting for their members under the guidance of the protection laws and they have an agreement with the National Trust, which I got for them many years ago. I found myself Chairman of the Wildfowl Association amongst other things. I think that we did a reasonable job in getting that organised. Many chaps still like to take a gun out for a Wigeon and a Mallard in the winter months.

Many other creatures used Blakeney. The Brent Goose could be shot in those days and many hundreds of them came in and fed on the Zostra Grass but I have proved that they prefer another weed called Entromorphia and also the mussel beds from which they could, at low tide, get various vegetation. Brents also like to feed nowadays on the tops of the saltings and the farmers' early wheat fields. The farmers get annoyed about this at times. Of course they are protected these days and there are many hundreds of these birds on Blakeney and other parts of the Norfolk coast.

So I had to get familiar with living with all these creatures winter and summer. One of my loves, as I have mentioned before, was sailing and I can't write memoirs without mentioning my exploits in dinghy sailing. The great day came when I suddenly realised that I had saved up enough money and my father said "Oh I will give you a bit more" and we will order a proper dinghy for you to sail in, a 14-foot clinker-built Starling built at Blakeney. The famous family of Starlings built all the clinker-built boats for the Blakeney sailing people and the gentry; they hired out the fishermen as their sailors and boatmen, and they bought these nice clinker-built boats, mainly for pleasure and also for the annual Regattas.

I eventually got my 14-foot dinghy which was designed on the lines of a 12-footer by the name of *Patheiner* which won many races. My old friend Will "Watch" Long used to sail down to the Point and have breakfast with the people he worked for, namely Madam Navaro and her son. She was a

My father with one of his tame Common Terns which nested around the same spot for many years. It wintered in West Africa.
My mother, who was scared of the water, gratefully arrives at the Point in my boat.

My first dog, Sherry.

Below:
My first boat c. *1929.*

Bottom:
Blakeney lifeboat **Caroline**
in 1918.

famous Opera Singer of many years ago and spent many weeks at Blakeney Hotel. Will Watch and his brothers served these various families, who had, some of them, private houses in Blakeney. He sailed them out to the Point and down the estuary. It was good to see them and they learnt me a lot, and I would never have been able to race (which I did many times with various craft and in particular my own) had it not been for the tuition of the Long family. My dear old friend George Long, the favourite of everybody who lived at Blakeney or knew Blakeney. George was a member of this famous family and he had many stories to tell, with marvellous expressions. He was a good Punt Gunner and very conscientious about wildlife as well.

I sailed other craft and eventually I did manage to win one or two races. I was keen as mustard and the greatest fun in those days was to see the competition, by two boatmen in particular, one lived in Morston, a fisherman by the name of Ted Buck. Ted was a good friend of the village of Morston and he caught mackerel and gave people fish for a feed now and again and he also kept us youngsters in order. He was very strict about behaviour in boats on Morston Creek in particular and he had his own mussel beds there. He had a great rival in the sailing world and that was Will "Watch" Long who sailed for Navaro. Will and Ted had great rivalries in sailing and Ted Buck sailed a boat for the local farmer in Morston Mr. Stratton, and his craft's name was *Double Chance*, a second boat which was overhauled and refitted. Very fast indeed, I think she was about 18–20 feet if I remember rightly, a sort of half decker.

The other craft at Blakeney I can't remember, *Seagull* was one I know and another craft was *Hermine*. Clinker-built again and built by the Starling family made specially for racing in Blakeney Harbour, where they knew they had local competitors. The Starling built boats like to hold the cups because of their tradition I suppose and it was good fun to watch these craft. Then along came International Dinghies. I was very lucky to obtain an old boat, an International 14-footer, which I had many happy hours in. The fast International Dinghies were very exciting to watch. These dinghies had their own particular race. The Blakeney Sailing Club was eventually formed and other competitors came. Sir Peter Scott sailed a lot in Blakeney in his younger days. He was very keen and he went out with members of the Long Family shooting in the winter months.

Great International races were held in Blakeney in those days. I can just remember in my early youth watching these from our Lifeboat House on Blakeney Point. We watched them go round the buoy and then we would rush up to Blakeney in the evening to see the other races that were going on. Anything from swimming to rowing plus more sailing. As time went on another event was gradually formed and this was a rather lovely traditional race between Morston and Blakeney. At the end of the season it became a

19

tradition that the last race of the season officially in Blakeney Harbour was the Morston Regatta, which meant that we took our boats to Blakeney. I eventually became sort of commodore of this event, I had my old 12-bore with lots of blank cartridges, to see them off. We started with a handicap from Blakeney and had a long course which finished at Morston. We had a race round behind the lot with my motor boat in the latter days to catch up with them and get to the finishing post, before the first boat got there, and then we graded out the various firsts and seconds, according to class and we gave some nice little cups and various awards. Before I was honoured to be acting commodore or starter, I used to participate and I was very lucky to win the Helen Turner Cup which was a memorial cup.

A very well known sailor, Helen Turner was a native of Morston Village, her father was a farmer there and she was marvellously keen, like her sisters. She was "top notch" amongst the women sailors and she loved every minute of it. Another well known gentleman and highly respected National Dinghy sailor was Peter Catling from Cley, originally a schoolmaster. He was indeed the king pin of dinghy sailors in Blakeney Harbour, he taught many of us a trick or two in creek sailing. At the age of nineteen I was thinking "what time will I have for all this, if I am to be Warden I will not be able to get away and sail so much as I did in the past", but things worked out reasonably well.

Going back before my father died so tragically, and suddenly, he and I had some marvellous exploits. We used to do a bit of beach combing, because beach combing was part of tradition as well as a living for some of the local people of Cley and Blakeney. They got some handy pieces of wood which they would sell or use themselves. These which washed off the deck cargoes of craft going along the coast in rough weather, they very often lost a few dozen planks or more and various different things came in. My father did his patrol one morning (I didn't get out too early) and he suddenly appeared carrying a box full of oranges, eating one at the same time, and he said "boy come on quick there is a beach full of oranges". They were quite nice Spanish oranges, not one but many thousands of oranges along the coast of Norfolk, way past Weybourne and Cromer. They were either dumped or washed off a Spanish ship which was bringing this cargo to Britain. It was during the Spanish Civil War and somehow they "got wrong" with either their dealers or somebody or other and they dumped their cargoes (so we were told) and all these orange boxes broke up in the sea and scattered along the beaches. My father was a hefty chap and liked fruit. He and I went along the beach and we gathered boxes and boxes. My mother made lots of lovely marmalade and the fishermen came and collected them because my father gave them the wink straight away and said "look there is plenty of stuff on the beach", and over came the fishermen and helped themselves like many other commodities that came in at times. The only problem was, of course, my father and I having filled ourselves with oranges from morning to night finished up trotting to the lavatory for about a week! so we paid for our fruitful sins.

Many stories can be told of this consignment of flotsam and so these memories stick in one's mind when you sit and think and there I was with all these early incidences behind me awaiting to start a career in charge of this wonderful spot of Blakeney. My father being a Devonshire man and ex-navy he was a good cook actually and he loved to cook our lunch or dinner on the Point when my mother was either ashore or busy. In the winter months we went across killing rabbits and clearing up the place and he would cook a meal for us and whatever member of the family was with us, my uncles or anybody else accompanying us that day or weekend. On one occasion I remember that we were there with an uncle of mine on holiday from London and he liked his food a lot. He loved a good feed and knew my father could dish up a good meal. He heard my father say "we're getting really short of meat, but I will see what I can do today. I had wanted to make some Teddie Oggies". How many people who live in Norfolk or elsewhere and Devon would know what he meant. They were a wonderful Cornish or Devon pasty which were nicknamed in Devon "Teddie Oggies". It meant that they had taters and various meat in them. They were lovely Cornish or Devon pasties if you like and my father had an expression of saying "well how big one do you want, boy, do you want a four oarmark one or a six oarmark one" and when he said "oarmark" he meant that he would put a thumb-mark when they press the pasties together. When they have been made and thumb-marks so many inches apart meant that the more thumb-marks you had the longer the pastry was, and he called them "oarmarks" like a rowing-hole and said that it was where the oars used to be struck through when you rowed it.

All these marvellous expressions from Devon came out invariably. But on this occasion when he had to find us some grub, we came back in after messing about in the hills and he had all these lovely pasties cooked and my uncle said "Well where did you get the meat from, Billie. I thought you didn't have any meat." "Well," he said, "I went onto the beach and there was this old seal laying there and I thought well he's dead now I'll take his liver out, so I took his liver out and made these pasties." Of course this was a tall story, a fib, but after he told my uncle, he didn't want any pasties and that was rather amusing because he liked his food and he was a very good chap at eating pasties usually. I'm afraid on that particular occasion he was put off completely, so there was more for the rest of us. And so these little incidences went on, all kind of merriment, during our work and play if you like.

Many stories can be told about wildfowling. I remember many times coming back wet through and cold with no ducks and nothing to eat or nothing to present my mother and father. A good wildfowler put up with the bad nights when there were no birds about and he took the smooth with the rough. My old friend George Long was a marvellous Punter and I went across the Point one morning to look at my traps early and I found a 12-bore gun laying on the shingle which the tide would obviously cover when it came up at the side of the creek and I thought Good God somebody's been messing around and have either been drowned and dropped the gun or else they have thrown it away, or it had fallen out of a boat. I couldn't make out what had happened, so I took the gun ashore and took it to Stratton Long who was a nephew of George and knew every gun in the District. "Well," he said, "that's old George's gun – blast how did he come to lose that." So I said, "Well I had better take it up to his house." "Don't you do that," he said. "If you go up there and he ain't there and Mally is there (his wife) she'll shoot the poor old boy when he comes home for losing it." "So," he said, "you had better give it to me and I'll tell George when I see him that I've got it."

A few days later I realised what had happened. Stratton said that George had gone ashore early just after daylight to clean his punt out and get ready to do some stalking and he had unconsciously laid his 12-bore gun on the shingles, because they always carried a handgun with them in the punt to kill any wounded birds which had got away. Yes, these Punt Gunners were very conscientious, if they had a shot and didn't kill the bird cleanly they would make sure that they were killed by the handgun, because the duck was worth a couple of bob or so in those days and that was their living. In fact old George recalled that when he was younger living with his brothers in Blakeney that "in them days boy my father had to go out and shoot a few Knot before we could eat, before we had any grub". A Knot is a small wading bird which again is protected these days but there were once many thousands which flew about in flocks and they were a good eating bird, they were bigger than a Snipe. That was the food of the local people on the foreshore in those very early days.

Stratton Long and Walter are great pals of mine and Stratton is a bit of a character as well, sort of one of the leading lights in Blakeney. Walter and his wife kept the White Horse pub after Walter's parents died, but since we are talking about wildfowlers talk about these particular couple wildfowling, because they, like me, were brought up with a gun. This particular night Stratton and Walter thought they would go down to the North Side or as we call it Flight. The Wigeon were flighting in with a nice east wind, which is the correct wind to try and get an odd brace or two as they fly through from west to east into the wind. You can get a good clean shot and Stratton and Walter were flighting duck as we call it, sitting down in a quickly scraped hollow or in a small creek out of the way with just head and shoulders above the marsh so that they could swing their gun onto a duck. Stratton heard

Walter having one or two shots and thought "Hello there, they started to come in now." As the wind got a bit stronger, suddenly Stratton looked up and thought "blast it's snowing", flakes kept going past him and he couldn't make it out at all. The sky was clear there shouldn't be any snow. Then suddenly realised that they were feathers and when he contacted his brother after the shoot was over and he said, "I don't know, there were a lot of feathers about." "Well," Walter said, "it was me plucking the birds. I shot a couple and I thought I would pass the time away and pluck them before we went home," and this was the reason why Stratton was covered with snow – or feathers as I should say. All these funny little stories come to light, but nevertheless it makes amusement especially in the pub a week or two after, when you would have a drink together and somebody would start pulling another's leg. For many years after Stratton had a job to live that one down.

There weren't many geese really. There were a few Pink Footed Geese that came along but we were never too lucky with geese at Blakeney, they used to like the Pink Footed Geese to feed on the new lays on the farms and they used to flight out to Stiffkey Sands and in the olden days there were quite a lot of geese shot when they flew out from the land or vice versa onto the land in the mornings to feed. They were a wonderful eating goose, the Pink Footed Goose, unlike the old Brent that were a bit strong and "sea-weedy" unless you knew how to cook them and could kill that strong taste. The women got to know how to treat this goose when they cooked it.

Another bird which was very plentiful and migrated every autumn (September was a fantastic month) was the Green Plover, or Lapwing or Peewit. Thousands of them flew to the west in September and if you got a westerly wind you could guarantee that these flocks of birds would flock along the coast. They were difficult to shoot but they were a marvellous eating bird – two or three of those in a pie and you had a good lunch. Again the women of the household knew exactly how to cook them. My mother was a "dabhand" of course as she was brought up to it and she could make a Lapwing or Peewit taste like a Pheasant. Another bird we must not forget, because it was the poor man's game (technically it was a game bird) was the Woodcock. Some of them would nest in Britain like a Plover but the Woodcocks leave us in summer and mainly come back in the autumn. The true and definite sort of date to look out for Woodcock is the first moon in November with a north-east wind and then you automatically hunt the sand dunes on the foreshore or the marshes or the mainland in the early mornings and these Woodcock would drop in out of the sky and they sit there and get as stiff as boards as they have flown a long way and you would flush them out and they would flop up in front of you, not like the fresh speedy Woodcock that twists and turns normally.

Even so they are hard to hit and every wildfowler and local gunner would try to get a brace of Woodcock when they came in. Sometimes you were lucky and there was a good fall of them and a dozen or so could be shot. They were difficult to hit despite the fact that they were tired. In sand dunes they were marvellous birds, they would jump up at your feet sometimes or a dog would put them out fairly near where they had been nesting and they would twist and turn over the top of the hill and you would have a job to hit them first barrel. Many many cartridges have been wasted on Woodcock, including mine. They had a wonderful habit really because if you missed them with both barrels, they would whiz over the top of the hill in front of you and as soon as they lost sight of you over a sand dune they would drop down again. So you knew exactly where they would be sitting when you wanted another go at them. Load-up and you would stalk them and up they would get again and then you would waste two or more cartridges and so on. I never did get the knack of shooting Woodcock.

As time drifted on, having been appointed Warden, I looked back on some of my father's exploits, in fact how he was appointed to the place. There was a character in our village by the name of Major Philip Hamond, who was the village squire really, everything that went on in the village was referred to the major, because he helped everybody if he could, a very tough sort of chap, but nevertheless he was a great friend to everybody and he also respected ex-servicemen very highly, being an ex-serviceman himself of the Boer War and Great War. He was a marvellous character and he more or less got my father the job on Blakeney Point. My father put in for the job but had to have references. Major Hamond was on the Committee for the National Trust Management at the time and he said, "I'll do my best for you, Billy, I think that you should have the job, you know about every inch of it, being coast guard in the village originally." My father got the job, thanks I think to Major Hamond. Likewise he supported me when I was appointed Warden. He was a real seaman, he used to go sea fishing in his own boats, bringing in a load of mackerel. He loved to go to sea and he actually had his honeymoon on one of the old boats (in the middle of Morston Marshes) that used to trade in and out of Blakeney Harbour, the *Blue Jacket*, which was a houseboat he bought and converted in the early days. All sorts of tales can be told about the major in the village and many of us ex-servicemen were expected to go and see him when we came home on leave and if you didn't you would be in trouble because he would love to have you in and give you a bottle of beer and ask where you'd been. This was one of the duties you had to do when you came back for a weekend or week's leave, he wanted to know how things were going on. He was a big noise in the Home Guard because of his past war and service record, he was ideally suited to command a section of the Home Guard in the district.

One character who supported me and another chap I must never forget was Reggie Gaze, a little fellow who helped my father. He was there with the original Warden Bob Pinchen for a time and he used to frequent Blakeney Point a lot with his camera, he was a terrific photographer and in the early days he took some marvellous photographs which are in the reports of the National Trust Blakeney Point during Professor Oliver's time. Professor Oliver had many of his photographs in later years. Reggie loved to put his little hides up to conceal himself for his photography in amongst the nesting birds and I will always remember helping him to make the hides. He favoured a very slender sort of square shape hide with a few poles about 4 or 5 foot high odd and about 4 foot square and Reggie would sit in there for hours upon end and film Ring Plovers or take still pictures of them with his massive old camera, a big box camera type with a plate which he developed when he got back to Norwich. He could run off terrific prints from those plates of his and he taught me all sorts of stunts in dealing with wildlife when you are filming, how to respect them, and how to deceive the birds when you made a hide and went in to photograph from it. You never went in just on your own, you always took somebody to the hide with you, "because" Reggie used to say, "these birds can't count, if you take a mate with you and you get in the hide and tell your mate to walk away when you are comfortable, the old bird thinks that nobody is there then and she'll come back to her nest immediately and you can film her or photograph her as much as you like, unless of course you do something silly and let her see your fingers or something through the slit in the hide, which will give the game away. If you do that you have a handkerchief which you can stick through the hole in the top of the hide and you can signal to your mate who is sitting way back watching you through a pair of binoculars to come and approach the hide again and just to let the old bird think that there is nobody there by coming to the hide and returning again."

All these dodges you had to learn, noting the exact distance, checking the wind and we had to be very careful about disturbing birds in the height of their incubation, because in a dense colony of Terns one had to be very careful, especially if you had any opposition nesting near like a Blackheaded Gull nesting in a clump about 20–30 feet away from the Common Tern. If she had a chance this old Gull would pinch an egg or even a chick, because they were barbarous neighbours to have. I had no respect for them when they were nesting and neither did the Terns of course. A gull would get in some way or other and play havoc if you allowed him to. I had to cull or keep the numbers down as much as possible, after proving to the powers that be, that these gulls were destroying the Terns, disturbing them and taking their eggs and chicks. Too many Blackheaded Gulls were very bad indeed for a nesting colony of Terns.

Ring Plovers came in for the same treatment because the Plovers were quite defenceless. These little Ring Plovers nested along the beaches and various valleys along the Point and they were quite vulnerable to the gulls who were continually hawking for titbits. They would watch a Ring Plover run off a nest and swoop down and try and find her eggs. In my first year on the Point as Warden I had a grandfather still alive, he was Head Keeper of Bayfield Estate in his early days. He was delighted when I invited him to come across and give me a hand in the nesting season with the visitors. I would appoint him as sort of a "Static Information Post" where he hadn't got too much walking to do and when I was busy showing people around he could collect other people and give them a chat about different things and show them a few odd things in the vicinity.

We had an old houseboat in those days on the end of the Point, which was called *The Caretaker* which my father had to use as his sleeping quarters in the height of the season. It was because the far Point, as we still call it, was quite a large expanse of young dunes and it was essential to be out there away from Lifeboat House at certain times during the nesting season because people would try to pinch eggs or disturb them and it was obviously easier to sleep in the old boat and keep an eye on things during the night. Everybody enjoyed that time as well because they were fascinated by this system of control, although I wasn't because in those days visitors could walk where they liked and I after a few years realised that, as Professor Oliver predicted, more and more people came and the only protection that we had was to show people around carefully. They could wander through the nesting grounds, which were very large and extensive. Nearly every nest was marked by a stick which in the early days as I said I had to chop for my father to mark as the Terns laid their eggs. This was not a very satisfactory situation. Time went on and summer went, the nesting season was over and the next thing I knew war had broken out.

Top:
*Sheringham lifeboat **Man-chester Unity of Oddfellows** with Cox'n "Joyfull" West in charge entering Blakeney Harbour with **Mona** in tow, August '63.*

Left:
***Yankee**, c. 1886, her remains can still be seen at the Point.*

Below:
Cley Quay and windmill a century ago.

Left:
*My mentor, Prof. F. W. Oliver, who negotiated the gift of Blakeney Point to the
National Trust in 1912.*

Right:
*Maj. P. Hamond, notable resident of Morston, involved with the running of the sanctuary
at the Point from its early days.*

Below:
Reginald Gaze, professional wildlife photographer, with my father. He was also Assistant Warden.

2 | Wartime Adventures, New Zealand

I was called up in October 1939 to join the navy. I joined the Navy Reserve of course and off I went. Those were hectic days for everybody in uniform as well as at home. I spent my early training in a marvellous seaside resort at Skegness, the Butlin's Holiday Camp of all places, we took it over immediately and we were there for six or seven weeks getting uniforms sorted out, a bit of squad drill and, the biggest joke of all, was that they had a couple of dinghy whalers, navy whalers rather, which were a six-oar job or a seven-oar job and a coxswain. They had these on the bathing pools and of course I was taught to row which was a big joke! They tried to teach me to row and of course I knew far more than they would ever know about rowing, so I put up with it and we finished up back in our respective divisions.

I was "appointed" which we all laughed about, us chaps from Norfolk were sent down to Devonshire, Devonport of all places and so we had to go there and finish our training, and take up whatever we wanted or thought we could do in the navy. We were all ordinary seamen, we passed out eventually as able seamen. I suddenly got a draft notice, which meant that I had to go and join a ship at last, with my friends and pals, one or two from Norfolk, who trained with me. We found ourselves off to London to join a New Zealand Liner the *Rangitata* and we were put aboard her as passengers, about twenty of us, and we had to mix with many New Zealanders going back to their native land. We were about the only gang of uniformed people who were on board this lovely liner, with all these very nice people who had more money than we did, and we did volunteer to do a few jobs. They had a lot of stuff to shift in the way of cargo in the holds, so we would give the staff a hand when we could and we took turns on the after gun for a defence purpose. This was a gun which many merchant liners had on the stern of the ship with a trained crew to have a go at a submarine if they were attacked at any time. So we used to do watches on that and then we used to be entertained by these very nice people going back home to New Zealand.

Through the Panama Canal, another experience. Eight weeks it took us to get there by convoy and zigzagging and we got down to Auckland to join a cruiser. This was a rather new type of cruiser to us, she was an ex-Blue Funnel Liner. She was fitted with gun emplacements although she was a cargo ship. The Alfred Holt Line and the Blue Funnel Line were also subsidised to be built extra strong in case of war and they were converted to an armed merchant cruiser with half a dozen six-inch guns and plenty of depth charges. We should have picked her up in Auckland shouldn't we, but oh no, typical naval routine, we found that she had not been in Auckland for some time, she was in "Windy" Wellington, having a few repairs done. So we had to take a trip from Auckland to Wellington by train, 800 miles, which was a hell of an experience to us raw recruits.

On our first step ashore I had a pound note in my back pocket, which my old man always used to say, "Always carry a quid in your back locker boy and you can't go wrong." I had this quid and I said to my mates, "Come on let's go and taste the beer." So we went into a hotel bar called Gleesons Hotel in Auckland, we got a marvellous reception. I put the English pound note on the table for a few half pints and the barman said, "We don't call them pints here, mate, do you come from the Old Country?" I said, "Yes." "Well," he said, "sit you down, we'll get you some beer." So we did and he called out some various people who came from Norfolk and Wales and we had some miners with us and ex-miners, we were home from home literally. New Zealanders I will have a life-long respect for and a few days later we had to take this long train journey down to Wellington.

"Windy" Wellington, how true it was. The wind never stopped blowing and we soon realised that we were about to start our naval career in earnest when we saw this large 12,000-ton armed merchant cruiser laying in dry dock. Our first job was to report aboard and we found ourselves painting the bottom of this great ship the next day. Much to the disgust of some of the lads who joined up with me, they had never seen a paintbrush in their lives but I was quite at home. Of course we met many New Zealanders after that and we were always in and out of their harbours, but during our stay in Wellington we got to know several people ashore. And so after a few weeks aboard this armed merchant cruiser, we were floated off from dry dock and we spent many weeks and months around New Zealand in and out of various ports.

We met again people who were on board the liner coming over, who lived here, fruit farmers in particular. We found that some of our ship's company, who had been in and out of Wellington before we joined the ship, had been ashore to help these farmers to repair their tractors and make spare parts for them, because there was a short supply of spares for the old Fordson tractors. In return these very kind people used to supply us with boxes of apples, delicious New Zealand apples, and we were also invited to the farms and taught how to ride their ponies, although I wasn't terribly good at that game. You finished up with some sore behinds, but nevertheless this was our memory of Wellington, "Windy" Wellington.

The pubs were very generous to everybody and I think that they closed about tea-time. During the period when we were there Dunkirk fell. There was a wartime map in every pub, people grieved for our losses and our defeat and for several days after Dunkirk fell we couldn't get a drink ashore as the pubs were more or less closed in mourning. New Zealanders were loyal to the last degree. One or two nice little jobs we had were to take the New Zealand garrisons fresh supplies, and relieve the troops with a fresh number of soldiers, and bring back the ones who had done a duty on various islands. One in particular was Pitcairn Island, the famous island of *Mutiny on the Bounty* and we took supplies there and stopped a couple of days and enjoyed their hospitality. The natives were very very loyal to the British Crown and everyone of these little old huts, which were straw huts where the natives lived, had a picture of one of our members of the Royal Family. Very touching.

I sent a cablegram back because this was a cable station, and a very important one where all the transatlantic and pacific lines met. We were invited to send cables home to our nearest relations and next of kin. I sent my mother a cable to say that all was well. I daren't say where I was because of censorship and I said "Happy Birthday" on the 13th May, it was about the 11th May when I sent it. I was delighted to be able to do so and for years afterwards when I got home it was a big joke because my mother produced a marvellous greetings cablegram addressed to her from Cocos Island with my message typed on the bottom, which just goes to show how lackadaisical the censorship was even in the heights of war, because she knew straight away where I was. I got letters back to say "Are you enjoying New Zealand" and I couldn't make out how she knew where I was. That is how I found out.

And so we enjoyed our hospitality in New Zealand, we never had any troubles until we left the place. One particular journey which I really enjoyed was up through the short fjords to a lovely little wool town called Timaru, and when we arrived at this "Quayside" where all the ships apparently took the wool from that particular part of New Zealand, we were made so welcome. The inhabitants of Timaru invited us to a social dance and get together and they cleared their wool barn and produced music for us to enjoy ourselves with their company. We went to one very prominent tourist attraction called Rotorua, where the hot springs were. It was exciting, all these large hot springs which were produced there, and the locals utilised these hot springs for hot water for their central heating, it was a marvellous idea because it was scolding hot from these underground volcanic springs.

Eventually Italy came into the war and we were immediately called up to the Indian Ocean to do some real naval work, we had to go into action or do some patrolling and convoying in a danger zone. Our headquarters were in Bombay and there we picked up various convoys, some of them up from Australia. We used to go and meet them off the Australian coast, the *Aquatania* and *Mauritania*, which were troopships. They carried two or three thousand army boys from Australia and we had to escort them up to the Middle East. We used to do a circular tour, Colombo, Bombay, Karachi, Aden, Mombasa and back to perhaps Durban and then across to our base at Bombay again, because there was always a danger of a radar-armed merchant battle cruiser which was raiding the areas, and trying to sink the odd merchant ship which it did on occasions.

I should have mentioned the fact that we arrived in New Zealand soon after the *Achilles* had arrived back from the Battle of the River Plate in which *Exeter* and *Ajax* and *Achilles* achieved a great success, they sank the *Graf Spey* which was a battleship from the German navy. There was radar in that part of the ocean and it did a lot of damage and helped to sink a lot of merchant ships. The *Exeter* was badly damaged; actually we saw her before we left Britain. She came into Devonport with great holes in her from the nine- or eleven-inch guns that the *Graf Spey* had shot at her in battle. When the *Achilles* arrived we were told by our ship's company that they had to give the *Achilles* crew a hand in parading through Auckland to celebrate their victory and great times were had by all.

We had some exciting times going from Bombay and around the Indian Ocean into Aden. We caught up with an Italian submarine after she had been escorted into Aden and captured. Depth charges had to be dropped here and there to sort things out now and again. Aden was a rotten old place, it was very hot but we did get some sailing there, we could take our whalers out and sail when we were in harbour. It was quite a good idea for that and it kept us a little bit cooler than usual.

We picked up various bits of information. Crete had fallen and a destroyer by the name of *Kelvin* limped into Aden from the battle in which the *Kelly* under Lord Louis Mountbatten was sunk. We read about this everywhere afterwards and I was lent to the *Kelvin*, where they told me all the exploits they had been through. We also got some photographs of the invasion by the German parachutists on Crete, Suda Bay, which I treasure today, because they were developed by our ship's photographer. We got some good accounts of what went on in that dramatic period.

We went back to guard Colombo and other places and this is where we copped it. On the 1st April 1942, Easter Sunday of all days, we were expecting the Japs, because they had had a good go at Singapore and we had been trying to evacuate odds and sods from there. We were chased back to Colombo because we knew that the Japs had got a strong fleet of aircraft carriers and they actually raided Colombo on that particular day in 1942. I will always remember that day because we were sitting peacefully at anchor, Guard Ship, we were told we were anti-aircraft defence. The *Dorchester* and *Cornwall* had been sunk a couple of days or so beforehand, two super cruisers, and we looked up into the sky and saw all these aircraft turning around high up. We said to each other, "Oh good God the R.A.F. are here at last what a good job, they'll sort things out for us," but "hold you on" as we say in Norfolk, down these beggars came. They were "Stukas"!

We managed to get a few of them, in fact the anti-aircraft thought they shot down about fifty, but they got us well and truly. Two or three down the funnel and we were ablaze and sinking at anchor, not a very pleasant situation. My job was torpedoman and as I was aboard that cruiser, I had to cut all depth charges loose before they were hit by a bomb and also take all the primers out so that they would not explode under water.

We found ourselves survivors in Colombo, we lost several of our shipmates I'm sad to say and we eventually were detailed to take small craft away from Colombo. They wanted it evacuated because they thought that the Japs were going to invade Ceylon at any moment. We were detailed to take a small boom vessel (a boom defence vessel, which was designed to look after the board mines on the boom of the entrance of the harbour to guard against invasion). Off we went, we had to get to Bombay we were told so we steamed off at about two knots. The boat was a coal burner and was very hot. We had two or three natives down below in the engine-room and four or five others on deck to navigate. We got to a place called Coochin, as we were getting short of grub. We had a couple of days there because we did not want to stop too long when we discovered, or it looked to us, that about seventy-five per cent of the population had Elephantitis. We daren't take any food except from other ships who were kind enough to give us some tinned grub. The natives were trying to flog us duck eggs and all sorts of things, and we daren't buy from them because of catching this horrible disease. Our fresh water came from another ship as well as ships' biscuits.

Off we went on our way around the coast to Bombay. When we eventually arrived we were shipped back to Britain on a troopship, *Aquatania*, a four-funnelled liner which was not all that pleasant as there were too many of us aboard. I went down with jaundice and arriving back in Britain went on foreign service leave for five weeks. I spent most of this time in bed recovering from my illness, and that is how I found myself back home. I put in for an electrical course. A seaman torpedoman is an electrical engineer aboard a ship and I put in for the higher rank of Leading Torpedo Operator which meant that I was, or had to be, qualified in a school of electrical work in Chatham to which I went.

I got assigned to a brand new ship eventually and then I thought, "Well, I don't know, should I go to her or not." I then put in for a mechanics course because they wanted mechanics very badly for generating the electricity for a very specialised job on Fleet Sweepers. These were little destroyer-like vessels, small ones about 2,000 tons, and they had a very special job. They had this anti-magnetic mine sweeping gear aboard them which meant that you towed two electrodes on the back of these little ships and you generated high voltage every few seconds to create a magnetic field behind your ship, the ship being neutralised from magnetism beforehand by a band around it which avoided any chance of setting off a mine. We went over mines and the field which our electrodes created behind us exploded them. It was a very intricate and specialised job so I went for that particular grade and went to a brand new Fleet Sweeper which was just being completed in Belfast.

While there we tried all their Guinness which I didn't like very much, but we had to accept the hospitality. We were then sent up north to Tobermory, where we were on a practice course, to see how we could get on. The whole ship's company were trained to get us to the ship. We were put through various tests and courses until we were qualified to do our job properly. It was there we joined our flotilla (the Tenth Flotilla) of Fleet Sweepers. We were sweeping out of Scapa Flow to Norway and we had to take our craft ahead of the fleet. The raiding aircraft carriers, they flew off aircraft to raid various ports which the Germans had occupied in Norway. This was a hazardous sort of job because if you got sunk in that part of the world you were specifically told not to search for survivors for more than ten minutes because the water was so cold you could not survive. This cheered us up enormously! We had to sweep ahead of these Fleet Sweepers and then they flew off the aircraft and raced back to Scapa Flow letting us get back as best we could behind them.

We had to endure all sorts of stunts like this, it was quite exciting at times. Then we went off across to Ostend and various spots which were then about to be reoccupied. Germany was crumbling by that time and this was all fun and games. Before I joined that particular ship, I had gone through for a mechanics course and prior to joining that ship I was on the Isle of Wight prior to D-Day on M.T.B.s. We had to maintain the craft that broke down on exercise. Before the invasion came we had an enjoyable time because we were not based on boats. They were moored in a secret area, a place called Wooton Creek, not far from Ryde on the Isle of Wight and we occupied a holiday camp. It was very nice and we all had our own chalets – home from home you might say. This was prior to the invasion of France and all sorts of characters were stationed there. All the barge crews from London came and they quickly converted to Royal Naval uniform – they had to during the war of course to fight with us. They were going to take the troops across in their barges and to be our escort, all sorts of stunts followed.

The doodle bugs started to come over for the first time and we had to catch one or two of those things when they dropped right near our camp. We eventually saw the R.A.F. sorting them out. All very exciting. As soon as D-Day had gone I found myself going to a new ship in Belfast as I said. H.M.S. *Hare* her name was – she was a little Fleet Sweeper. Very pleasant job really apart from one or two dangers. We used to go around to Harwich as well and I put in for various courses and unbeknown to me my skipper aboard that ship put me in for promotion to a Lieutenant Engineer so I had a pleasant surprise as we came into Harwich and I was detailed to pack my bag and hammock and go back to barracks and pass out for this commission. Victory Day was getting near so we were all full of the joys of spring. I found myself back in "Pompey" as we called it and we got stuck into the real shore-going life of the naval barracks which we thoroughly enjoyed. I was put in a mess which was far too small to hold all of us and we had to overcrowd each other a bit at mealtimes.

Then I was told that VE Day had arrived and we had to be dispersed. I said, "Why can't you demob me, I've got a job waiting for me." "Oh no," they said, "you must wait your turn," and I was sent up to Aberdeen to be in charge of the fishing trawlers which were converted to mine sweepers during the war and which were being sent back to their base at Aberdeen to be refitted back for fishing. All the gear from the fishing boats was dumped on the quay and dispersed eventually. The fisher-boys were delighted to come back to their old ships and take over. We were based with very nice people, there were several of us up there, I was based with a lady in Aberdeen, whose husband had been knocked about in the war very badly, in fact he couldn't walk, he was a cripple, so we were only too delighted to support her and board with her. We discovered all about the Scottish evenings and enjoyed the dancing up there.

Eventually I was demobbed and we found ourselves being given marvellous demob suits and we eventually arrived at our respective homes. An old pal of mine who was with me abroad, Walter Tubby, I still meet up with today. There was another character from Sheringham (his name was Bunkle). I haven't heard much about him since the war, but we were the three "Norfolkites" aboard H.M.S. *Hector*. Another character from Cromer who came and joined us during our commission, his name was Coleman, he got christened "Tubby" Coleman because of his size like "Tubby" from Caister who was very well built (we still communicate when we get a chance).

I can remember weekend leaves which amused me when we talk about "Dad's Navy" on Blakeney Point. The Coast Guard Service (consisted of the Long Family) with my uncle and another character by the name of Jack Woodget who was an ex-navy type. They had some wonderful times over there and we were roped in to join them when we had a weekend leave. They

35

would love you to go across and spend a night there, because this meant that they would have an extra member there who could go fishing with the chap off duty. There were two at a time on duty, but they did a watch each, so the one on watch would let his partner go off fishing with you. You more or less *had* to go because that is what they got you over there for, so I discovered, to go out and fish salmon and trout at night in the summer months. I had done it for many years before that, before the war, but to go back to the old routine with these lads was good fun. On one occasion they smoked my "duty frees" for me as hard as they could. After a couple of nights at the weekend I said, "All the cigarettes have gone, lads, you've smoked the lot." "Cigarettes you want?" they said. "Oh, there's plenty in that drawer." I pulled back the drawer in the kitchen and there was not *one* but about two or three hundred tins of cigarettes which were washed up on the beach from a ship which was sunk. These characters collected all these ship's cigarettes, mainly Players in fifty tins and they really pulled my leg.

They liked to do a bit of shooting and at certain times of the year you could get quite a lot of game. The woodcock, for instance, and duck used the place, we were all wildfowlers together. The woodcock were good fun. Although some of them bred in this country, as they still do, they were really migratory birds. They were a poor man's game if you like, they are on the game list today of course. If you got a north-east wind and you were there the first couple of weeks in November when these birds came through with a nice full moon, or a bit of a moon, you could always guarantee to find some birds resting on the Point after their long journey, or on the marshes. On this occasion Mathy Long and my uncle Trip Bean were on watch on the Point, suddenly realised that the wind and moon was right and this was November and that there would be some woodcock in. Sure enough Mathy kept watching from the lookout and saw a woodcock drop in on the sand dunes not far away and he said to Trip, "Look I've only got a few cartridges, boy, but I'm going to get a couple of woodcock – they will be nice to have for our rations," and off he went with his cartridges and gun. Trip recalls, "I suddenly heard bang bang and I thought hello, Mathy missed that one." Because if you have two shots it is a bad sign, it means that you have missed the bird, as a rule, because they are very crafty little birds although they are so very timid. They flop about in front of you and nip over the top of the hill and as soon as you are out of sight you can bet your life they are sitting there again. "Bang bang again," Trip said. Eventually after a lot of bangs Mathy came back with a long face and Trip said, "Did you get one?" "No, boy," he said, "I chased the ———— off the Point, he wouldn't come back here no more," and they are the sort of stories we used to get from these characters on the Point.

So my days in the navy had finished, the war had finished, the Point was handed back to the National Trust eventually and I had to take up my job as Warden. During the wartime the terns were reasonably looked after, admittedly the odd clutches of eggs that were laid earlier were made into pancakes by the Coast Guards on the Point, naturally of course as food was short. The odd clutch or two of terns' eggs were very useful at the beginning of the season when they were fresh. Gulls' eggs too, the Blackheaded gull was a delicacy, for many years after the war they were sold in London. The first clutches were gathered up and sold by the thousand to the London markets and various other parts of the country. And so I found myself back on the job at Blakeney.

Top:
Maj. Hamond's old house boat, ex-trader **Blue-jacket**.

Left:
Britannia, *ex-sailing drifter, ended her days as a house boat on the Point.*

Bottom:
The Warden's house boat **Caretaker**. *Grandfather Bob Bean and my father with cousin David.*

Winter work, trapping rabbits on the Point.

Like father, like son.

Top:
*The Italian cruiser **Barto-lomeo Colleoni** being sunk by shellfire from H.M.S. **Sidney** near Crete in 1940.*

Left:
*A near miss for H.M.S. **Illustrious** in the Red Sea in 1941.*

Below:
The battle for Crete. Suda Bay photographed by a New Zealand soldier. I never knew his name.

3 | Back to the Point, Eggs and Egg Collectors

Since I was demobbed on the 19th December 1945, I wasn't really needed to go back to the Point until the New Year at least. The real hard graft of Wardening is in the early spring. The Coast Guards had to be evacuated and the Point was sort of recognised once again. During the war one had to be very strict about who went over there and so things were a little bit humpty dumpty for the start.

I went over and killed a few rabbits and we got the house sorted out. My mother was a widow, you see, so she came over with me for my first year after the war, until I was married a few years later. I got things sorted out. She had left a lot of her furniture over there for the Coast Guards to use but we had to replenish a lot of stuff and get out all the old gear which mother had carefully hidden away for the war such as crockery for the Tea Room. The summer started, the nesting season started, I was rather looking forward to see what birds we had returning after the war. During the war as I said they were not terribly badly handled, the Coast Guard respected the wildlife as much as anybody else, as they were locals. Apart from the odd scrambled egg or two as I have already said they used to respect the terns and kill a few rats. I can't remember much about what really went on during the first few months.

My old friend Reggie Gaze from Norwich who was my great friend and tutor with regards to photography returned, and told us about his exploits during the war, and we had quite a lot of news to exchange. Reggie acted as my Assistant Warden (unpaid) because we wanted to re-establish his photography business on wildlife and other interests. The first year went fairly well. Lots of people came, the ferry wasn't really established and there weren't many boats usable because we had to get hold of a few old car engines and replenish the old engines to put more craft in the water and try and re-establish the communication.

Students occupied the hut for a short time, and Professor Oliver put in an appearance, and all was well I suppose at the time. It was very funny because the fishing was still pretty good and we had some good nights fishing just after the war. We pulled the Coast Guards' legs, and said, "Look, you didn't catch many fish, we got fifteen or twenty trout last night. What were you up to – sleeping off your watch for a while instead of getting on with some fishing?" But there it was. I had one big disappointment – the little lookout on top of the Lifeboat House, which had been put up by the Ministry of Transport, had to be taken down. This was a little six by ten sort of thing, a hut, which was useful to go up and look out and see what was going on all round. Apparently they had only borrowed it from someone, for the war so we were told, and it had to be sent back to its rightful owner – rather ridiculous but there it was. Nevertheless after a few years I persuaded the National Trust to let me put one up there again so we could have a good look round the place and watch for egg collectors, also we had to keep a weather eye out for people in trouble. This lookout is still there today.

All these tales I can relate as time goes on, but the biggest problem was of course to get re-established with everybody. I know one particular organisation that came along the beach before the war was the Holiday Fellowship, they brought parties along the beach and rode back on the ferry when they could, or vice versa and these re-established themselves and one or two new organisations sprang up and eventually our Point Sundays were a busy time again. Once the trippers came, then of course the ferry boats started running and more and more twenty-minute visitors came, and short-term visitors from Blakeney and Morston. If you knew the drill you would come down in the morning and go back at night, or get ferried across the channel at low tide by the Morston ferries, but that was the way of doing things if you knew Blakeney well enough to enjoy it all day.

There were plenty of shellfish around the place and lots of people enjoyed collecting their cockles. There were still plenty of flatfish in the harbour, such as butts, but this was a bit of a dying pastime because there was not quite the quantity of fish to be caught. I used to do a bit myself to get a feed for myself and members of the family from time to time.

Our hut had to be painted up of course and a few years later we got down to the regular routine. My mother was busy in her Tea Room and catering sort of started in earnest. Wages were not very high, not from the National Trust point of view. I don't know what I was getting a week, some little bit slightly higher than a farm labourer for seven days a week, twenty-four hours a day. We had to supplement our living as best we could. I used to do a bit of ferrying when I could and catch a few fish of course, rabbits were part of my pay in those days, like they were in my father's day and I had rather a nice steady time really.

It was realised after a bit that I did need an Assistant Warden, as there were so many people coming. The National Trust suddenly said, "Right, you can have somebody for a couple of months a year." Reggie Gaze promptly took over the assistant's job, because he was an unpaid one anyway, and I said, "Look, Reggie, you come and stick it out with me, you'll have to be my assistant proper," which he did, and he was very good at lecturing to the visitors. We had to take people round. Then we suddenly realised that we must do something about controlling the crowds, because this marking of individual nests was now beginning to prove to me, as I thought it would do, to be unsuccessful because there were too many people going round these nesting sites too often.

We suddenly hit on an idea, we had Stiffkey AA Camp, an Army Training Camp not far away. They were firing at targets all day long being towed by aircraft and on many occasions the targets were shot down and several hundred yards of wire was found washed up on the beach. It was like telephone wire to look at, it was covered and it was quite strong, and so we hit on an idea. I said, "Right, we will get a few good stakes and we will wire off one section of the terns' nesting ground, and see what the reaction is by the locals and the people who come to see them." We put a few notices up to tell people not to encroach over that wire instead of marking every nest. This we did and immediately I had a reaction from one of the fishermen. I assured him that it was a good way of keeping the terns protected because he got his living like a good many others did by bringing people down to see the terns nesting, and therefore he agreed, on condition that I took the wire down as soon as the nesting season had finished. Which I promised I would do, and so I did as long as I was there.

The Committee was then notified. Some Committee members could not make it out at all and, "Why can't we go and take our friends through the terns?" These were Committee members, mind you, and I said, "No, you've got to do the same as other people." In time we got to the stage where we could wire off more and more area and the terns were even more protected. Eventually when the material ceased to wash up on the beach from the army, who had, very conveniently, shot it down for us, we had to revert to the agricultural string which was quite good, the new ones especially, the red binder twine as we call it. This is still used today. This wiring-off system with a few pathways through it, for the fishermen to go through to the bay beyond the Point to get cockles and big worms worked, providing you thought of the local people and you got their co-operation. As Professor Oliver used to say, "Everything will be fine." I think it was.

We still had the old *Caretaker*, the houseboat where my father used to sleep and my grandfather of course was always coming across to give me a hand. He was my mainstay during the first year after the war as I have already said. With Reggie Gaze as well we were a good little team and eventually things began to change a bit because we got some very high tides and on one stormy night the sea covered the far end of the Point. That was in the early spring, January or February, and away went the old *Caretaker* and broke up on the Stiffkey sands somewhere. Our nesting ground which was quite unique on the end of the Point was more or less flattened so we had the terns returning to a sort of desolate piece of ground on that part of the nesting ground for a time and they returned back to the Headland as we call it where there was more dune space for them to nest and this meant a lot of complications.

We had a rather bigger area than we really wished to protect and guard because these terns were more scattered. The Sandwich Tern was our biggest headache. They were the large species which were nesting in Britain and they were very exciting really because people liked to see them because they are very prominent. Usually they made their nests in an area about two hundred yards square. This meant that though they were each apart they were very close to each other. Sometimes there would be as many as a thousand pairs. Luckily Sandwich Terns are very social birds. They had to be because when their chicks hatched out, which they do invariably in the same week as they all lay their eggs within two or three days of the same date, all these chicks hatch out together. You can on a good season see several hundred chicks, when they are seven or eight days old, trooping about the place. When they get older one or two parent birds sort of act as chaperon to them acting as guards, while the rest of the birds were out fishing, bringing food in continually to the chicks.

The amazing thing about it is that these birds can go round the flock with a fish in their mouths calling out and their young will shout out and they will give that fish to their own young and nobody elses in about several hundred chicks. I have sat and watched this for many hours and I was amazed to see how the chicks can recognise their parents. You would think that the parents recognise the chicks but they do not have to listen for their chicks to shout and this I have proved on many occasions. So the Sandwich Tern, although they are very fascinating and they need protection in Britain they are very unreliable because one year we can get a couple of thousand pairs at Blakeney and the following year my colleague at Scolt Head, Bob Chestney, would ring me up and say, Ted I've got all your terns this year, and he would have perhaps double the amount of Sandwich Terns on his place, which meant that we only had about fifty pairs on ours and this is how they fluctuate. They are very timid when they first arrive and you can disturb them if you unconsciously go near the nesting grounds before they lay their eggs and properly settle in and sit. So we would prepare the nesting grounds for visitors long before the terns arrive. Early May, the first week in May, the wire should be up and normally notices in position awaiting the arrival of these yearly visitors.

The most important member of the tern family is the Lesser Tern or the Little Tern. This is another creature which has come up quite well in my time, a very precious little bird. It has a nice white forehead and a yellow bill and flesh-coloured or red legs. Don't believe what the bird books tell you, every bird book that you pick up will tell you a Little Tern or a Lesser Tern has got yellow legs, they haven't, they have got flesh- or red-coloured legs. This again we can prove by the film or picture we have taken of them, sitting and watching them for hours. Why bird books should copy one another in their references I don't know.

Little Terns are very precious, really even today they get very badly looked after should I say because they are unlike the Sandwich Terns, they scatter down the beach and they like to spread themselves out fairly well. They like soft shingle and sand. So much so that very often they get too near the sea and they nest in a position where the high tides can wash their eggs out of the nest. They love soft shingle and sand and their eggs are very minute compared with the rest of the terns because these terns are quite small but very attractive. They are very fussy and I have filmed them several times. They bring in minute fish for a start to give their youngsters like all the other birds. Now and again you would notice that there was a young pair of birds obviously nesting for the first time and they would invariably bring in little shrimps and things which have got husks on and the chicks would refuse them, quite rightly, because if they do eat these little shrimps they can get caught in their gullets and they die. This we have proved on many occasions. These little birds soon learn the correct food to feed their chicks on.

I don't know what numbers there are on Blakeney now but when I left the place there was anything from a hundred and forty to a hundred and sixty pairs and they have come up from about twenty odd pairs in my father's time. We were very lucky to increase them because I think that this is due to the wiring off system again, they were not quite so vulnerable to people's feet as they were in the old days. It is very difficult to spot these eggs and as I said, they scattered down the beach very often and they would nest all the way along the spit towards Cley, right down past the Watch House. This is where one had to be careful to warn regulars not to tread on their nests. Unfortunately if you mark these nests in that part of the beach, egg collectors will look for them, see a stick or mark and they can find their nest quite easily. Through marking their nests from a safety point of view the egg collectors will come and take them from another point of view. They are very precious eggs, from Schedule One Birds which mean that they are on a special list of protection and the maximum penalty is quite high compared to those of ordinary birds' eggs.

So our seasons went from one to another. I haven't mentioned the old faithful tern yet, the Common Tern which established himself many years ago, I wouldn't like to say how many years ago, but way back before the place was protected, the Common Terns nested on those beaches and we used to average anything from 800 to 1,200 pairs of Common Terns nesting regularly. So regular in fact were these birds that they would come back to the same spot to nest. Pairs of birds would come year after year providing that same spot was still there. Again I proved this. I had one or two birds who got very very tame and I could literally approach them and have a yarn with them if you like, my father used to and you could see how tame they were by our picture in this book. One in particular I did go up to and nearly stroked her when she had got her chicks about hatched and she used to get very angry with me, but nevertheless she put up with me and this bird came back for many many years running. We did ring a few terns; this ringing system came into being after the war rather rigidly. It was there before the war of course but I used to ring a lot of terns for my father for a certain lady who was the official bird ringer at Blakeney and for the Trust. Some of the results were quite fascinating.

We proved that our Common Terns went to West Africa every winter. Lots of rings were returned from the Dakar Area of West Africa, and this was quite interesting. We never knew how long it took those creatures to get back to their winter quarters, quite a while I should imagine, but when I was in the navy of course during the war, I could see lots of terns about there in particular around Maldive Islands. There were lots of fascinating terns, one in particular the Fairy Tern which I shall talk about later on.

Anyway the Common Terns were our main stay. Whatever happened you could count on those creatures coming back in nearly the same numbers every year. Whitebait of course was their main food, where the Little Tern took smaller fish, perhaps because they were much smaller and they would take whitebait as well but the whitebait was the common food for the Common Terns – the old Sandwich Tern liked a Sand Eel if they could find them. Being a little bit larger they could dive a little deeper and from a greater height than the Common Terns. They fished as individuals, whereas the Common Terns fished in flocks when they were feeding on a shoal of whitebait. It was quite fascinating to watch the whitebait fishermen of Blakeney Harbour. Anybody who wanted to net whitebait would watch the terns and these old birds would tell them exactly where the shoals were by plunging in continually, which I expect many of you have seen.

Another bird which I have seen plenty of up north was the Arctic Tern. Arctic Terns, we had an odd two or three pairs, and recent years before I retired I proved on film that we had cross breeding. We had a pair of terns. One, the cock bird, was a Common Tern and the hen bird was an Arctic, quite fascinating to watch, because the Arctic Tern's egg is slightly larger and more round and has much darker marks as a rule. They are distinct, they lay out in the plain shingle whereas the Common Tern vary so much in their egg sizes and colour. I have had a clutch of light blue eggs on occasion and various other colours, a dark chocolate and a light blue egg in the same nest very often. Common Terns lay two or three eggs on average, sometimes four. The Sandwich Terns lay one and two eggs at the most, the Lesser Terns three eggs, occasionally four, and so it goes on. The most delicate tern which we used to pray to get nesting was the Roseate Tern, a lovely creature, a bit paler and rosier, hence her name or his name. On the breast of the cock bird you can see this slight flush in good plumage. They used to come, perhaps one or two pairs, in my father's time. I think the last pair I had nesting was around 1950. I filmed them up on the Farne Islands, little gangs of them there; there would be seven or eight pairs on the Inner Farnes and quite a little colony on the Lighthouse Rock, the Longstone Rock of the Farne Islands.

In Wales, in Anglesey, I went and helped to make a film of the Nature Reserve down there and the Warden come Director was a policeman. He was in charge of all this area and he allowed me to go out with a dinghy on the various islands in the estuary, and he said, "Go out and look at those Roseate Terns. I haven't counted them this year, Ted, go and see what you can find." Out we went and to my amazement there were seventy-odd pairs of Roseate Terns nesting on this small little rock. We were so excited, it was quite fascinating to watch, hearing their different calls and they had chicks hatching, so we could record this nice little surprise colony of Roseate Terns, which very few people I think realised how many there were. On my travels I discovered all these various creatures which I was brought up with on Blakeney.

We used to get all sorts of troubles, rats and stoats were another headache of course. A hedgehog could do a lot of damage, he would suck eggs in half a dozen nests a night and all you would find when a hedgehog had taken or eaten eggs would be little tiny bits of shell in the nests, which would give the game away. You knew then exactly who the culprit was. A rat would cart the eggs away into the marram grass not far away. As a rule you could follow his tracks and you would find half-eaten shells, half-eaten eggs, half-eaten chicks. Eventually if he had a hole he would have a litter of eggshells outside his hole. You could trap this chap that particular night because all you had to do was to put a trap in that particular run and you would bet your life that you would get him the next morning, but not before he had done a rather lot of damage, which was disappointing.

The biggest menace in the four-legged line was the stoats and that is why I used to partly keep my dogs with me all the time. Springer Spaniel and Labradors I had in the early years, and Golden Retrievers. My Springers proved to be the most efficient in latter years and I had one old girl, by the name of Sue, and her partner a young bitch Teasel, she would soon tell me where a stoat was. In fact these old stoats are so crafty that they would come along the beach and play and have their young up in the dunes; they would prey on the terns nesting, they would kill adult terns and drag them back to their dens, or perhaps eight or nine hundred yards up into the dunes, well away from the nesting grounds. They had this technique where they would never kill things on their doorsteps, but they would kill them away and then you wouldn't know where they actually lived. If you found things too near their burrows, they knew you would find them, so crafty were these creatures.

On this occasion old Sue told me where this pair of stoats was, so we set about digging them out and I took my gun with me as well and we got this old girl. I got her as she shot out of the hole after Sue started digging for her, she bolted out of another little hole at the top of the hill and I managed to shoot her. We carried on digging and we found nine young stoats in the hole, which we had to kill, of course, together with umpteen eggs and over twenty-three adult terns, many many chicks carcasses, but the terns had been dragged there half eaten by these little devils.

Our biggest capture, I think, was when my dogs told me that there was another litter of stoats about, two or three years before I retired and we went out looking for them and Sue told me where they were and we dug them out and found that they were too deep to get at. We dug two or three and so I trapped the burrows. There were umpteen holes, seven or eight holes all round this hill, where the stoats were going in and out like a rabbit would, only much smaller holes, in fact it was an old rabbit burrow which they had taken over. I trapped seven or eight stoats the next morning. They are easy creatures to trap, they are rather stupid with regards to traps. Providing you put the trap in their run and you know where they are working they are pretty easy to catch. I was delighted to get all this lot and you will see a picture of old Sue with her triumph and haul of stoats. This meant that we had saved several hundred chicks and adult birds from being killed on the nesting ground. Anybody who follows my footsteps I hope will take notice of various experiences that I have encountered.

One of the headaches that I had was the presence of Shorteared Owls, they can be a nuisance. They are protected you see. They nest in the mainland on the marshes, sometimes in an old rabbit hole in the bank somewhere they like to get, then these damn things would come across the harbour at night or just before dark, because they would hunt in partial daylight. They would surprise these poor old terns sitting on a nest because they would look down and see this black head bobbing about, the tern on the nest, and they are so sharp these owls when they are looking for things and they would dive down. The next day when you went round after an owl had been raiding your nesting ground you would find perhaps half a dozen tern heads which had been chopped off and two or three carcasses here and there, just the breast eaten and the rest of the body left. You get all these troubles from other creatures – people do not know or realise what some of these other birds which are quite innocent have to put up with.

Now we had rather an amazing thing happen a couple or three years before I retired. We suddenly realised a pair of kestrels used to come over during the daytime, an odd one or two and they would hover about and take the odd field mouse, or whatever they were after, even beetles. If they saw a chick they would have one as well; if they saw a chick running about the sand they would just drop on to him and away would go your chick, so I used to be very cautious about those creatures. We had a false roof in the old Lifeboat House, the house was lined out and the roof was all lined up with match boarding as we call it and the birds could go and nest in there. The starlings did in particular – they used to go in our false roof and on the end of the house. I suddenly realised that these kestrels were going into our roof. I said to my wife, "I can hear those birds up in the roof." You see they were scratching about there and talking to one another and I suddenly realised that there was a lot of business going on. They were nesting in our roof, right over our head, literally in our bedroom of all places, so the next day I lifted up one of the trapdoors that let you into the roof and shone a torch around. There, just hatching out, were four or five young kestrels. What was I going to do, there were bits of rabbit laying about the old birds had carted in.

Then I went out and watched her and my assistant said, "Those kestrels are pinching our chicks, you know, in broad daylight." I said, "Well they do hunt in daylight, of course they do." He said, "Right there's one now." I said "Yes" and they were carting off our little tern chicks which were nearly ready to fly – what were we going to do? So I got my shotgun out and every time they came anywhere near the nesting ground I would fire my gun loosely in the air, so as not to hit them but to put the wind up them, which it did a bit and then we suddenly thought of a bright idea. There are dozens of young rabbits in the hills, "Yes". So out we went and we killed at least two or three young rabbits every evening and we laid the young rabbit at the entrance of this kestrel's nesting hole, where he went into the roof; it was an access to the roof through a hole in the end of the hut. When the old bird came back she just took this rabbit in, thinking her mate had left it there and they fed their chicks from then on on our two or three or perhaps a week-old rabbits, which we supplied, and kept them away from our terneries by kidding them that one or the other parent had brought the rabbit in for the other one to feed the chicks with.

It was rather fascinating and we used it in one of the Survival films and we were quite satisfied because when the chicks were all out on the telegraph wire learning how to fly. One of them came to a dead end, he was a bit too cocky and he fell off his perch straight into our water tub of fresh water, the rainwater butt, and my assistant found him floundering about. He tried to recover him, but the chick actually drowned himself, so there were four chicks out of the five of those kestrels that hatched out and flew and we were very pleased to see these old birds taking their family back to the mainland out of the way, because we didn't want any more to do with them.

So you see the natural troubles that occur to a Warden I suppose, apart from the human egg collectors. There again egg collecting can be rather an experience, catching a cross-section of people, not just one type of person will take eggs, it was sad to say. I once caught an agent of the National Trust pinching or trying to pinch my Sandwich Tern eggs, and I discovered that he was an egg collector, because he had in his possession a couple of clutches of Crossbill eggs which he had had given or collected from Thetford Forest the day before he came to stay with me on Blakeney. This he admitted to. I gave him his marching orders, it was rather extraordinary that an ordinary employee could tell one of his employers to go and get off the ternery or nesting grounds, if not you would prosecute him. He did go right quickly I can assure you and I didn't see much of him because he retired from the job, after about two years. I never saw him after that unfortunate incident on Blakeney.

We have had all kinds of people try it on, people with camera of course is a favourite trick, especially a box camera where they can clip an egg inside the camera and pretend that they are taking a photograph of the terns. I had another chap and his wife march along the beach and I saw him stoop and pick up an egg and give it to his wife, she obviously hid it on her person and so when I approached them he said "I haven't got any eggs." "Well," I said, "your wife has." He knew well that I couldn't or daren't or wouldn't dare to search her though I was a Special Constable. Luckily for me there were a couple of ladies not far away sitting in one of my observatories, so I took this couple to them and I said to these two ladies, "Will you search this lady without us being present?" and they did and found not one but five or six eggs hidden away, one or two in her bra I think, which was a good capture because they got fined about £25 for egg stealing by the Holt magistrates a couple of months later.

I have had another chap come along the beach with his maates and come and ask me for a flask of water, which I gave him, and when he thought that I wasn't watching him he drank his flask of water and went back through the nesting grounds and put some eggs in this open flask, which he somehow concocted to hide eggs in. Another fellow I caught with a bird book, which had the middle cut out, to conceal eggs. A few pages either side can be stuck down to conceal them, you name it, we had it, we knew what to look for on various occasions. All concealments you could think of were used. My wife was very observant because being in the Tea Room we had a collection of birds and their eggs for people to look at and I used to say to her, "If you see somebody examining those eggs especially, give me a shout." So we had our land telephone, our ex-army telephone set from my wife's kitchen to our observatory, which was our own private line and she would give me a tinkle out there and tell me to look out for certain characters which she described. Many times it was through her information that we diverted another egg collector from pinching eggs.

Egg collecting seems to be dying out a bit these days, although you read of it. I think that the best catch we ever had was when I got a chap and his son with a haversack with 60-odd eggs in it, some of which were pinched off Cley Marshes. Billy Bishop, the warden there, he lost Reed Bunting and goose eggs, redshanks and all sorts of eggs that they were collecting.

Egg collectors can be pretty crafty after all we thought we knew about it. My father had a very clever idea which I have copied since he died. He said to me, "Boy if you get a Roseate Tern nesting here, you know what you want to do. If you get somebody watching this bird knowing that it has laid an egg and you think that they are going to pinch it, watch the bird down on the nest because these eggs are difficult to recognise from a Common Tern's at times. Once the egg collector sees the bird on the nest he will be delighted to pinch it if possible." So what my father put me up to was as soon as ever the Roseate Tern laid an egg and she had incubated it fairly well, you changed her egg for a Common Tern's from a nest some way away. You picked out a Common Tern with the same period of incubation as the Roseate Tern and you changed these eggs over temporarily until the eggs were about to hatch. Then you would change these eggs back to the rightful owner. If the egg collector pinched what he thought was a Roseate Tern's egg then he has taken a Common Tern's. So that is one trick to play on an ardent egg collector of tern's eggs especially.

So you had to be very very careful about all these dodgers. A question was asked me many times by various people, how do I tell a Common Tern from an Arctic Tern, during the nesting season especially. It has a simple answer actually, and I put it to them like this. If you approach a Common Tern's nest when she is hatching or about to hatch, they will rattle down at you like a machine-gun from the air, and crack you on the head if you don't bop your head quickly enough – very fierce characters when they know their chicks are about to hatch or even if they have got chicks they get quite as mad. But on the other hand if you approach an Arctic Tern's nest and she is in the same position as the Common Tern (i.e. about to hatch or she has got chicks), you get an almighty crack on the head (or on the skull as we say in Norfolk) and then she will "shout" about it afterwards and tell you what she

51

has done. So you get this silent attack from the Arctic Terns and you cannot get away very often without being hit.

I used to always have my stick over my shoulder so that the birds could not hit my head. They would perhaps just miss the top of the stick when they wanted to attack me, when I went in to examine a nest or to look for vermin. The Terns would attack me as well as anybody else, they were very untrust-worthy and rightly so. Billy Bishop and I had our own private system of warning each other about egg collectors, either coming my way or egg collectors going back to Cley along the beach. On several occasions Billy brought a policeman down Cley Beach after I had tipped him off that there was a chap collecting eggs and they caught several people like that arriving at Cley from Blakeney Point along the beach, unconsciously going to their cars and Billy and the policeman would apprehend them and catch them with either eggs they had pinched from Blakeney or Cley the day before. So we had this very convenient arrangement.

4 | Schools, Celebrities, Shooting Parties

The Point was used for educational purposes and several schools used the Point for outside academic instruction, as the Educational Authority liked to call it. As the post-war period went on more schools wished to use our facilities. One school in particular which I cannot write a book without mentioning is Runton Hill School, a public school for girls. They used to come to Blakeney Point before my father and mother were in residence over there, the previous Warden and his wife entertained the school once a year, they had what they called their Blakeney Day. This meant that just before they broke up for their summer holidays and finished that term, partly to celebrate their success in examinations they came to Blakeney in full strength, the headteacher and all her staff and most of the girls, as many as a hundred people, all ages of course at that school. They would arrange with me when I came over to pick the right time by the tides; they came down at low water and across the marshes and my cousins and I ferried them over at low tide and took them back on the high tide after tea in the evening.

My mother in those days, and later my wife, had to provide tea for them in the Tea Room, this was the tradition, ever since the Tea Room existed for the Runton Hill School. They had a marvellous headteacher. The girls were very well disciplined and it was really amusing to watch this headteacher. She would come outside the Tea Room and blow one long blast on her whistle and all these girls would sit up like spaniels trained to the gun and listen to what her instructions were. Some of the girls wanted to go round the nesting grounds with me, other girls went off with their respective teachers to study plant life and geology of the site and they went down into the dunes and on the beach. The rest of the girls had their special little spots in the dunes to laze about and picnic until it was teatime and they all assembled back in the Lifeboat House for their tea altogether. It was their Blakeney Day, a free day if you like, they could more or less do as they wished. It was marvellous really to see these young ladies doing what they wanted.

Today that school no longer has a Blakeney Day. They ceased this annual outing before we retired from the Point, I am sad to say, because I know they all enjoyed it and many of the girls have told me since that they sadly missed this last day of their school year.

Another school, a public school again, a boys' school which is well known of course is Gresham School at Holt, they too used Blakeney. They used it thoroughly and properly I should say, because they had a superb master who brought individual groups to study ornithology and geography mainly. A chap called Mr. Ramidge was their teacher; he was strict with the lads he brought and the boys were well behaved. They were not a bit like the girls, as regards freedom, whereas the girls would jump up to their waists in water and get to a boat to clamber aboard it, three at a time, the boys had to have a plank of wood and a box to stand on. They were very very particular, they didn't want to get their shoes muddy or feet even wet. This always amused me and my cousins, who saw the difference in the boys and girls behaviour. The girls couldn't care about getting wet feet, whereas these boys were so particular.

Anyhow they, I am sure, enjoyed the place and they learnt a lot and then as time went on they came with a particular master from that school who became well known, a great friend of mine, Dick Bagnall-Oakley, a marvellous photographer. It was his main hobby because I think he was a history master technically, but he used the Point with two or three keen members of his school, youngsters who wanted to learn photography and take up ornithology a bit, and I used to put a hide or two up for him when I was quite young. I used to watch his technique of photography and Reggie Gaze would compare notes as well, with regards to how he and Dick used different lenses, techniques were discussed and prints exchanged and this is how I learnt the technique of filming wildlife.

Eventually I took up this profession under the guidance of Reggie Gaze and one or two of the other people who I watched, in particular Dick Oakley. He was a still photographer in the early days and then he changed to ciné. And so all these experiences taught me much and I learnt from other people's mistakes as well as my own. We just had these public schools coming at first and then as the time progressed the state schools had more outside instruction and they could afford to help finance outside trips to Blakeney and other places of interest.

I suddenly realised that I was getting six or seven local East Anglian schools, Norfolk schools in particular on one day, and none the next. I thought that this had got to be sorted out somehow and I contacted the Assistant Chief Education Officer for Norfolk and I said, "Look, you communicate with your schools once a month I know, through a news-sheet perhaps you could add some advice about visiting Blakeney Point. Would you ask your teachers to get in touch with me beforehand and I will plan out the best day for them to come and the tides and all the rest of it." He very kindly did this and this helped a lot, the schools enjoyed the Point even more because I could instruct them when to come and have not more than three schools a day if possible.

So the visits increased, not only from Norfolk but we got Leicester Education Authority sending children and Suffolk and Essex, even Lincolnshire. They came from very many parts of Britain. The schools from far away, eventually started booking up to stay at the various hostels along the coast so that they had plenty of time to sort out their visits to various places. The Youth Centre at Sheringham was very very good and very useful to these schools and they took parties in for a week at a time, giving them various days out along the coast. The Norfolk schools I got to know terribly well. I used to send a report back to the Education Officer every year in Norwich and he suddenly said, "Look we are going to give the National Trust one hundred and fifty pounds a year towards your outside academic instruction for our schools as it is so successful." I was delighted, of course, as a hundred and fifty pounds a year to the National Trust Management Committee to help run Blakeney Point was very useful. This went on for several years and I used to send my report to the Committee and the agent would send it off to the Education Office and they in turn would send them a cheque.

But unfortunately one agent forgot to send my report one year and so the grant suddenly ceased except for what the schools would give in their own generosity in the collection-box at Blakeney Point. But nevertheless we had a good system, I thought so anyway. They used to come on the ferries at a reduced price in the early days. It was one shilling and sixpence a head return I think for a child in a school party, and my mother and then my wife in turn provided cups of tea and lemonade and sold the odd fancy sweets or packets of crisps. The financial benefit was quite good to everyone concerned. One school party we had caused me a lot of worry; their teacher would bring them as he said to blow off steam. This annoyed me because a Nature Reserve was not meant for people to blow off steam, especially during the nesting season and on one occasion I found him under a pile of boys on the beach and all these boys were trying to hold him down, quite near the nesting grounds making a lot of row. On another occasion they used to jump off the sand dunes and I looked out of my lookout window and saw seven or eight boys, quite young, carrying another boy to the house and he was bleeding from the mouth. I rushed downstairs to see what was happening and the boys said, "Oh he jumped off the sand dunes, sir, and he has cut his tongue," and I discovered that he had bitten his tongue right through. I said "Where is your master?" "Oh," they said, "he's up in the hills – he told us to bring him to you." This to my mind was not terribly good with regards to the welfare of masters and children together, so we had to rush this lad ashore to the nearest doctor and I don't know where he went from then on, but I was rather annoyed with this behaviour. These are the sort of incidents that used to make me realise how the behaviour of certain people changed over the years on Blakeney.

Some teachers amused me because though there were very many good teachers there were a few not so good. To give you one instance, I used to like to listen to the teachers and after I had chatted to her or his school party for a quarter of an hour and took them around, sometimes the teachers would have to start off on their own because I was busy with another school and on one occasion I walked up behind a teacher who was showing her class a Ring Plover's nest, which we mark individually along the beach because these creatures nested away from the ternery very often and they were all marked with a ring of stones or by four sticks and a wire around them to stop people treading on them. On this occasion this dear lady was describing the nest and then she said, "Isn't it marvellous how a little tiny bird put those great big stones around the nest." This brought the house down when I told this to my assistants and other friends at dinner that night. This little bird as she described it, he wouldn't even be able to pick up a cockleshell hardly, without having a job, let alone a great big flint stone which weighed about ten times as much as the bird. This lady thought that these little birds had placed these large flint stones around her particular nest.

Some of the geography teachers were superb and I had some marvellous maps sent to me, expertly done, of the changes of the various areas on the Point. The schools who really wanted to go to town on geography and the changes of the shingle beaches I advised and persuaded to come and do their work in the autumn term, possibly mid-September, because then all the terns had finished nesting and gone back to their winter quarters, we hoped, in Africa. This meant that the whole of the Point was free for the teachers and the keen types of children who wanted to spend the day mapping and measuring the various areas, which had changed over the years, or in that particular year after a storm. So great use was made of Blakeney Point and still is I hope of all the different subjects which can be studied.

Another creature we haven't mentioned was the seal. They have increased so much so that I think there is rather a serious problem with controlling them. Many years ago, before the war, seals were looked upon as a fish eater taking lots of flatfish in the harbour which people relied upon for their living, and other fish as well. These old seals would obviously eat some and they were frowned upon and in the early days you could get ten shillings a nose for a seal. If you killed a seal and cut his nose off you could get ten shillings from the Ministry of Fisheries. As time went on the controversy increased about

My wife feeding a sick Guillemot with Sand Eels.

*Salvage timber from **Zore**, a Swedish boat which came to grief in the 1950s.*

Bottom left:
Auxiliary coastguards (Dad's Coastguards) on duty at the Point in WW II.

Bottom right:
"Drawing the shore" for Sea Trout. Billy Bishop and I with the largest specimens ever caught in one night

what these seals were doing and so the Ministry of Fisheries and Agriculture sent their own investigators down and they employed a couple of fishermen to go and kill ten or fifteen seals and when they killed these seals these scientists took the stomachs out of the seals and their contents and analysed them and they discovered and informed us that of the seals that they had examined the majority of them had been eating whelks and other shellfish. There are thousands of shellfish just outside in the sea, where these seals would dive.

Up north I have filmed them with their pups, they are delightful creatures, these grey seal pups, but before I retired we realised that we had got one or two greys at Blakeney. A grey seal bull in particular was quite prominent. Percy Trett, a great friend of mine takes a great interest in Scroby Sands. There is a small colony of grey seals out there and we went out when they had got their pups. We made quite a nice little film of these dozen or less grey seal cows with their pups and the odd bull or two was in the vicinity, watching out. The grey seal bull has two or three cows or more in his harem, and they mate as soon as the pups are born. There's what we call a delayed pregnancy, like some other creatures such as stoats. They will mate and their pregnancy will be delayed for a month or two or perhaps half a year before they start producing pups. It was quite interesting to go and see grey seal pups in Norfolk. I had seen hundreds of them on the Farne Islands and now of course I think that there are more and more every year in Norfolk.

This is great entertainment to the visitors at Blakeney especially, they run boat-loads of trippers down just to see the seals. Some of them don't even land on Blakeney Point, these people just get the ferry boats to take them down to enjoy a trip around the end of the Point where the seals lie basking on the sandbanks or the flood tide.

Somebody asked me about the old wrecks on Blakeney Point, the remains of the old trading ships that came into Blakeney when it was a port many years ago and the fishing vessels. Two in particular on Blakeney Point. The old *Yankee* was a trading vessel in and out of Blakeney and she finished up on the beach as a houseboat and a home for Professor Hart and his large family of boys. He had four or five to my knowledge at least. The old *Britannia* lies there too, now she was a deep-sea herring fishing-boat, or so I was told, a very deep craft, she and two or three others would sail away from the Sheringham area and go away for several weeks and come back with a load of fish, usually I think herring salted down, and then they discharged their loads and off they would go again. This old boat was a well-known relic on Blakeney Point – when I first remember her she was a well-kept houseboat. The first warden lived in it for a time on Blakeney Point until the Lifeboat House was converted to the Warden's quarters and then he left the old *Britannia* and resided in the Lifeboat House, which is there today of course.

The *Britannia*, when I knew it, was owned by a Captain Lloyd and another friend of his who lived at Taverham Mill near Norwich, a lovely old spot. Captain Lloyd and my father were great friends and my uncle and father spent many an hour on the *Britannia*. He was always worrying about the high tide flooding the old boat because she would lay on that marsh, and as I said she had a very deep keel on her and she had to be propped up with bilge-keels as we call them, extra chocks at each side of her to keep her upright when the tide was out or when there was no water around her. This was many weeks a year because only the fortnightly tides came anywhere near her on the marsh, near Pinchens Creek, a creek where we land people. The *Britannia* was docked there on the marsh itself and so all sorts of bright ideas my father and Captain Lloyd concocted to pull this old boat higher up every time there was a big tide at high tide. They were praying for big tides so that they could get her well above the average tide. This they did by putting umpteen empty wooden barrels all round her, close to the keel and making them fast temporarily with rope and when the tide came up, of course, they lifted her a bit earlier than usual. They did eventually get her up by that method and the block and tackle on the bow with a large anchor way up on the beach so that they could winch her up if they didn't manage to float her or partly float her.

One occasion which I shall never forget because I went aboard her with them this particular night and a very high tide we prayed for and the tide passed over and we got her up a little way and the tide went out and they said "Well it is nearly midnight now, we will stick it out". Captain Lloyd said, "Have my bottle, Billie, and we will get out heads down for the night." This was during the winter months and I was with them, so we just rolled into our respective bunks, I left my father and Captain Lloyd nattering over a tot of whisky or whatever they were drinking and I woke up about an hour or two later. My father said, "Well that's d——— funny, isn't it marvellous how those stars are shining through the top hatchway there." So Captain Lloyd looked up and said, "Stars, Billie, they're lights, what the devil's happening?" And of course what had happened was that one of the chocks which kept the old boat upright had washed away and she had laid over on her side at a very steep angle and what we were looking at was Blakeney Hotel lights across the channel! That indicated to me that they had really had a good go at this bottle of whatever it was, because they didn't realise the steep slope of the floor or the deck that they were sitting on had gone down to forty-five degrees nearly, and the lights of course were shining brightly through the top hatch, because they were now level with eye sight of the foreshore.

All these things that have happened, one thinks about and records in one's mind, but this one will stick forever. It took some living down because the next day they had to go ashore and get some great big jacks from the local farmer to jack this old boat upright again and then put her chocks in the rightful position before the next tide arrived, because had they not done so the tide would have flooded this old boat out really severely and all the dry gear which was aboard would have been not very dry by the time the tide had finished with it.

So that is one of the stories about the *Britannia*. She now remains on the Point, a few ribs only and a little bit of keel, I think, is all you can see of her because she gradually broke up. During the last war especially, she was in a bad way.

The *Yankee* was a steel boat, there are still remains of her today and Professor Hart and Professor Oliver of course were great friends because they had the similar subjects they used to study in common and they would meet on her. Another professor from the London University was staying with Professor Oliver, and accepted an invitation to go across this little bit of marsh to where the *Yankee* was moored. Professor Hart said "Come and join us for dinner with Professor Oliver", and the story goes that my father looked out of the kitchen door and saw two objects going across the marsh, Professor Oliver in his Blakeney Point attire and an old pair of canvas shoes and his trousers rolled up, but Professor Salisbury, a colleague of Professor Oliver, was all dolled up in his dinner jacket, he had to take his evening shoes off apparently and roll up his best trousers and plough across the muddy creeks in that attire, which really amused everybody. Not very often do you see people in dinner jackets and bow-ties on Blakeney Point.

5 | Filming, Television, Travels and Tragedies at Home

Apart from being a prominent member on the Management Committee, Captain Lloyd loved shooting. He was, to my mind, a typical Norfolk naturalist. A sportsman come naturalist, he would look after things that need looking after with regards to various creatures nesting and breeding around him on his estate, and at the same time like many others he liked to shoot a duck or pheasant.

To my mind these people did more for conservation than people realise today. He used to go up the marsh and flight a widgeon and I used to go with him and take my dog and pick up the bird he had shot, because they are pretty difficult if you haven't got a good dog and you are flighting duck when it is just about dark, especially in a gale, or wind, or rain. Very often you have got a job to find these ducks when they fall out of the sky and drop into a creek or a load of marsh bushes or other vegetation. It is quite difficult to find a bird in such territory but a dog will pick it up in a matter of minutes.

I had some good dogs, my old pal Sherry was my first love of a dog really. He was brought up on Blakeney as a puppy and was given to me by a gamekeeper from Southrepps who worked for Captain Lloyd's father. The dog was sherry coloured so we called him Sherry. He was a cross between a black and golden labrador which made him that colour, a throw-back. A very intelligent dog, he would tell me where various things were, in the way of rats and stoats and then he would come with me nearly every morning to fetch the mail from Morston Village, especially at low water as he loved to swim. We would go across the harbour at low tide in the dinghy and he would be ahead of me, a marvellous swimmer. It was only a matter of about three hundred yards across the channel at low tide but he would beat me, and off we would go to the village and pick up the milk and bread and other stores that my mother needed.

In those days, of course, I am talking of well before the war when I was a youngster. Sherry loved to carry the *Eastern Daily Press* back ahead of me. He would literally swim across the harbour with that paper with his head held high, so as not to get it wet and this we sort of trained him to do when he was a pup. He cottoned onto that and very very seldom would you get a wet *Eastern Daily Press*. He used to tear ahead of me. As soon as he saw that I was just about to land on the side with my dinghy, he was waiting for me on the sand and off he would go up to the house to give my father or mother the paper before I got there. That was the sort of dog he was, he would guard me and some of my cousins who came to stay with me, he loved children and he would watch us when we were swimming. When we were out anywhere he would always come and sit and watch us. I then got him to swim out very often and grab the rope of the dinghy which was anchored just out of my reach. This saved me from taking my trousers off and wading in to pick up the dinghy. I could get Sherry to swim out and grab hold of the anchor rope, there was a good length of line on it and he would pull the dinghy in just enough for me to get hold of it, without filling my waterboots up.

All those sort of tricks this dog was so superb at, and he would sit and watch for a stoat for many hours. He would sit on the edge of the ternery and if he knew that there was a stoat working you'd bet your life that he would have that before dark because he would sit and wait until that old stoat worked on a nest and he would have it straight away. I eventually went in, after the war, for a Golden Retriever, there again because I was given a magnificent pup by one of my friends and I kept that bitch and bred from her and everybody loved my Golden Retrievers.

Apart from working on Blakeney Point there were many jobs to do with dogs on the mainland. Various gamekeepers gradually realised that I had some reasonable dogs and as years went on I found myself being invited out on a Saturday, especially to a pheasant shoot, to pick up all the wounded birds and the birds that the guns had shot and couldn't find. This was called "picking up", actually a local term for a person who was responsible for finding wounded and dead birds which the guns were shooting and dropping behind them and very often couldn't find and so this was quite good training for a dog. It was a good day's work for me as they paid me an extra bit like the beaters who beat the pheasants out of the woods and over the guns, with the gamekeepers in charge. I got paid the same wage as a beater and I always, in recent years anyway, had a brace of pheasants on a big day for the use of the dog, so my dogs earned their keep picking up pheasants, and other ways as well, and this was good experience.

My best loved estate was perhaps Bayfield, because Bayfield Hall was where my grandfather was head keeper many years back. My mother was born on that estate, many times she had told me about the time when her father was keeper and she and her brothers and sisters were taken to a Holt school by a very special carriage which Sir Alfred Jodrell provided. As years went by I was "picking up" for various estates and I went and picked up at Bayfield quite regularly for a dear old gamekeeper friend of mine Billy Palmer, who was a superb keeper and a superb naturalist. He respected a lot of creatures and showed me a lot of birds that I had not even seen nesting, and he also pointed out various ways of showing where different members of the vermin family had done their work overnight. He could tell if a fox had been at work, or a stoat, at just a glance at whatever the creatures had left, half eaten or skinned. He had lots of nice nests for me to look at in latter years and he allowed me to go and film various birds nesting in the covers and woods around the hall at Bayfield.

I used to pick up very very regularly and we had another treat with regards to shooting. When the season of pheasant had more or less ended, the estate owner always instructed his keepers to have what he called a cock shoot. This meant that everybody who had helped during the shooting season to pick up birds, and other gamekeepers who had assisted in the shooting days on that estate were invited by the estate owner and the gamekeeper of that estate to have the last shoot of the season. It was always a cock shoot, you were not allowed to shoot hen birds, you just shot the cock birds which you could hunt that day. A similar system to the pheasant shooting routine was worked. You have several beaters and guns and you sort of drew lots to have the privilege of standing where the governors used to stand in the big days and shoot their hens and cocks. You were allowed to take a stand once or twice during the day and have pheasant driven over you, which was a great privilege. I never got many cock birds, perhaps seventy or eighty on a big estate all day long was a good score of birds, but nevertheless it was a very enjoyable day and we shot rabbits and a few hares which had to be kept down in numbers and we finished up usually at the local pub for a quiet one, to celebrate the day.

Another marvellous shooting area of course is Holkham, and Billy Bishop, like me a warden, had a similar sort of routine. Billy did a lot of loading. This means that when the gentleman shooting as a guest on the estate itself, had double guns, two 12-bore guns, he had a man with him to load the second gun, so when he had a double barrel at a pheasant and another one then came quickly he just changed the guns over with his loader who was standing behind him. This was a rather special job until you got to know how to do it. You had to be a bit careful and we did a lot of this eventually.

I used to load as well as take my dogs with me and by the latter part of my experience as warden on Blakeney I went in for Springer Spaniels. Springer Spaniels I have mentioned before, they told me where the stoats were, they were superb little dogs for picking up at a big shoot, everybody loved to watch my spaniels at work. A great old friend of mine is Tom Savory of Cley who was my solicitor and my mother's solicitor for donkey's years. He invited me to go out with him picking up because he liked someone to help him with his gun and we went to Lord Walpole's about every other Wednesday through the winter. He would ring me up and say, "Come on, Ted, we have got another shoot on the Wednesday", and off we would go.

This was good fun. He liked me to support him and he was very grateful if you said, "Look up, there's one coming." He perhaps didn't spot it and I was experienced of course whereby Tom hadn't had as many days out in the shooting field as I had, because I was going from one estate to another during the winter months to supplement the low wages from the National Trust. I needed more money, especially as I was paying a mortgage on a house I'd just had built. You couldn't do anything else but try and earn extra money; this was recognised by the Management Committee because I put in so many hours in the summertime that you were allowed at least two or three days a week to earn money elsewhere during the winter months.

There are many stories to be told about shooting at Holkham, this wonderful park with farms all around it, which fascinated many shooting people as well as conservationists today. Billy Bishop was an old hand at loading, for many years before I took up this occupation in my spare time as an interest. Billy could tell lots of stories about various members of the country's nobility that he used to meet there and load for actually. Even a lot of the members of our Royal Family shot there, King George VI on occasions.

One good story was told about Billy; he was loading on this particular day for one of his regular gentlemen who he could be quite open with, and use typical Billy Bishop phrases as we say. This gentleman was a walking gun as we call it, he was detailed to walk with the beaters because the long strip of woodland or belts as we call them along the walls or long narrow woodlands which hold a lot of pheasants and other game birds had to be driven out by the beaters perhaps a quarter of a mile walk and driving these birds forward all the while to the guns at the other end. Some of these birds broke out to the left and right, so there was what we called a walking gun either side of the line of beaters to shoot at the birds which escaped to the left or right of the drive. As well as pheasants and woodcock and stuff that flew out there was always a rabbit or two and several hares. On this occasion Billy was carrying a spare gun for the gentleman he was loading for and carrying bits and pieces like the odd pheasant or two that was shot whilst walking, and a hare or two. Billy had a couple of pheasants, and a hare, and his gun, and it was quite a weight to carry time he had walked the whole length of this drive. Out came another hare and then another one and Billy shouted out "Too far, sir, too far, don't shoot" and this gentleman turned to Billy and he said, "Too far, Billy?, but I could have shot that easily, it was well in range." "Oh well it was too far for me to carry it," he said, and that is one of the stories that Billy had his leg pulled about. It is quite true. Everybody took it in good part and of course this would be one of the shooting stories at dinner you could bet your life.

After a day's shooting these gentlemen would relate some of these stories to their fellow guests. There were a lot of woodcock over for the winter. Holkham was a good place for woodcock when they were "in" as we said, and on shooting days sometimes twenty or thirty could be shot during the day. There was a special prize given to the gun, gentleman gunner or the chap who could kill two woodcock, one with each barrel without dropping his gun down, that is to say he swung onto a woodcock and shot it with his right barrel and immediately another one flew out he would swing onto that and shoot that with his left barrel, without dropping his gun to the normal position and this was a very difficult thing to do. If one of the guns did that years ago I would sign a witness paper, because if they could get a couple of witnesses to say "Yes, that was true, this chap did shoot two woodcock right and left", without any hesitation he would then apply to the makers of Bols Gin and get a bottle of Bols Gin free, for this achievement. How true that was I never did find out, but I have never heard of anybody getting this bottle of gin, but I have witnessed it once or twice during my many years of watching people shoot whilst picking up and loading.

Partridges were another famous sport in Norfolk. In the olden days, partridge shooting was very popular because many farms had little cover for pheasants, not so many woods as some places and so that was classed as good partridge country, nice light soil with plenty of barley stubble and a few root fields, which partridges liked to feed in. Classic shooting all around at Holkham. The farms that Lord Leicester owned were farmed by tenant farmers usually, and the shooting was preserved for his Lordship of course and his guests. The gamekeepers had to look after all the game on the farm as well and there were about eight gamekeepers employed on the Holkham Estate to my knowledge in the early days when I was loading there. These chaps would assist their colleagues on shooting days and then when they shot the farms for partridges this was another exciting day, very quick and alert you had to be when you were loading because partridges were driven over the hedge to where the guns were standing, off a root field preferably; sometimes just off stubbles.

These partridges flew over in their coveys of anything from half-a-dozen to fifteen to twenty and a good gun would try and get a right and left shot, like you would at woodcock, first one barrel and then the other. The chap who was loading would have to be very quick to put a gun into his hand quickly and take the empty one away and so on and this was very exciting. I was loading for a gentleman on one occasion and we had a lot of birds that day and the last drive was really exciting, and you always took care when loading for a gentleman not to run out of cartridges, and you had a huge bag of cartridges and a beltful perhaps. On this occasion when we had finished shooting that day I had three cartridges left in the bag and I began to sweat I can tell you before we actually finished shooting. I thought that any minute now we were going to run out of cartridges and I would look a proper charlie – apart from that I wouldn't have been thought much of as a loader.

The places where you think about when you have done a lot of loading and shooting are the obvious places where sport was good, and when I say sport I don't mean just lots of birds flying at you. I mean birds that came out very high and were very difficult to shoot. All the difficult angles which these guns had to try and shoot these birds and the speed that they flew was part of the skill and the sport, you didn't just go and shoot a bird as soon as it got off the ground. If you could help it you had it driven over and this was part of the sporting gesture and the love of shooting came into that.

Bayfield Hall was a fascinating place. The Bayfield Estate as I have mentioned many times before had some marvellous birds from those high hills, pheasants were driven out and the guns stood down in the valleys and this was real sporting shooting. Stiffkey Valley was another lovely place to shoot. In the olden days we were told that the early estate owners many many years ago planned out the planting of these woods especially for shooting and holding the pheasants in these high woods and encouraging them to breed and live in there and they would then give some superb sporting shots in future years.

This is what has happened if you look carefully at the various estates. They have all been planned out very carefully generations ago with regards to the sporting side of it. Stiffkey Valley or Stiffkey Farms is now owned by Lord Buxton, a great old friend of mine and of many other people who I shall mention again no doubt before I finish my book. The Stiffkey Estate was exciting in different ways because of the valleys there. In one particular valley the meadows in front of the north side were an excellent place for snipe as well, because snipe are good sport if they are driven properly and these were the sort of mixed shooting days you had on these estates. You could have a snipe drive if you felt like it when there were a lot of snipe in, and ducks would flight through there in the evening. There was a special duck flight area, where you could again enjoy an evening's duck shooting, preferably after a day's pheasant shooting. The host would invite you to stop and have a cup of tea and then go out and flight a few ducks for half an hour just before dark, just to finish off the day and then you would have dinner of course with your host before you departed. This was a typical shooting day.

Apart from these estates for the shooting aspect there was a terrific lot of wildlife, Holkham in fact was a fascinating place to know, a lot of history to relate, with which I am not as well conversant as I would like to be. The memories I have are many and great because I used to spend my latter years by filming there. A large flock of Canada Geese used Holkham. I am told

Mid June at the Point.

A family of Lesser Terns, early June.

Some of the colony of Common Seals which breed on the point.

one of the earlier Lord Leicesters introduced them into the country, they are not really a British goose of course. They were introduced in Britain and they have spread all around the place now and many estates have got little flocks of Canadas. They nest at Holkham and then spread and nest up into Lincolnshire and various other parts and come back in winter on the lake at Holkham. They flight out and feed on the meadowlands and around the farms and they get sorted out by the farmers if they are a nuisance on a wheat field. Early spring wheat they have to be chased off, because they can do a bit of damage if they are left to feed continually on a field of growing barley or wheat, but these very large old geese are very noisy and they are quite fascinating to watch and of course they fly all around Holkham Park.

Another thing which many people enjoy when they drive through are the herds of deer, again when there is snow and ice on the ground. To watch them down by the lake with the flocks of geese all around them makes a fantastic picture and these are the sort of things that live in one's memory for ever. Thank God we had these large estates created by what I call people who are or were, still are, the foundation for conservation. Lots of conservationists as they still call themselves wouldn't agree with that, but it is very very true. If we hadn't had these estates formed and gamekeepered, protected not just for shooting but for conservation, some species would be obliterated. That is my whole argument, certain creatures must be controlled to help other creatures survive, and not just the vermin, the rats and the stoats, but there are other birds which like to eat other birds and so forth. If we allowed hundreds of jays and magpies to dominate the woods there wouldn't be any small birds left and hardly any other creature would survive in the woods, hence the common sense of the early conservationists, the landowners and the estate owners which we in Britain inherited. I hope that this will be realised more and more as we suddenly realise that certain bodies of people try to create nature reserves and they haven't got a clue how to control a certain species. They believe that if everything is left it will be a wonderful nature reserve, that is just where they are wrong, if it was left for everything to do as it liked there would be a domination of one species and not another and so on.

The years after the war became more and more enjoyable as time went on. Billy Bishop became gamekeeper for the Cley Hall Estate (as well as warden for the marsh) and there again I went over on shooting days and helped him when they had their own little shoots over there. Major Blount was a prominent resident of Cley, he owned Cley Hall. He came from Leicestershire, I think, he was the High Sheriff in that part of the world and then he returned to Cley because his family and relations had a foothold there. The old mill at Cley was a family seat and he became Chairman of the Local Management Committee at Blakeney Point for a time. Although he and I didn't always agree on every point and every subject with regards how to manage Blakeney, I don't think that many committees and I did agree on everything because it was obvious that I had the experience and they thought that they had, but we had some good fun.

Billy and I, in our shooting days, and one of the earlier memories that I have of Cley Marsh and also of Hickling was that in those days the coots were a bit of a nuisance, or reckoned to be, and they used to have their annual coot shoot at Hickling. Several hundreds of coots were shot on this particular day or two every year. It was properly organised, the coots were driven over the guns who were sitting in punts on the rivers and creeks. The coots were driven out of the reed-beds by beaters or keepers; they didn't take much disturbing, they soon flew and they were very high fliers. They used to go up and fly over the guns pretty high and we had an annual coot shoot at Cley in those days as well, which Billy Bishop organised on behalf of the Norfolk Naturalists Trust. Now of course there is no such thing, it is all protected and there is a ban against shooting.

I suppose the coots are still breeding just as much on the broads. In Holland, of course, there are thousands of them. I have seen them, but that was another sport or tradition which has died, out, partly through conservation and bird protection acts and partly through the numbers I think being reduced by other methods. There was another fascinating estate where hundreds of pheasants were reared, not only were the pheasants allowed to breed in the wild on these estates, of course they had to be reared as well. Lots of pheasants are rather stupid and the hen birds laid their eggs in each other's nests and all sorts of nonsense. They laid them in stupid places, so the gamekeepers, as part of their job, had to collect a lot of early eggs which were laid haphazardly and they would put them under hens or bantams and hatch them out like that. The gamekeepers would hand rear these young pheasants, so that when we talk about rearing pheasants that is how it was done.

Today I think they buy a lot of already hatched chicks and rear them the easy way, but in the olden days the gamekeepers had to have a lot of old hens. They used to go and buy up sitting hens, which were broody and let them sit on pheasant eggs and hatch them out for them. That was one way of doing it and this increased the population of the pheasants the following year for shooting.

Kelling Hall was a fascinating shooting estate as well and I knew the keeper there very well and again I was asked to load or pick up there. My old friend Tom Savory used to get invited there and he would say, "Come on, Ted" and off we would go again and we would have a day there with my dogs as well, my two spaniels. On one occasion we were shooting a bit of bracken off one of the hills, we were standing down in this little valley and my two

71

A Sandwich Tern chick.

Some of the estimated 3,000 Sandwich Terns who nest on the Point.

Sue.

...are Fairy Terns on the ...land of Gan in the Indian ...cean.

Dropping in for tea with Stanley Webster, whitebait fisherman.

...Morston Regatta (the battle ...Morston Creek), the last ...ce of the season in Septem-...r.

spaniels were sitting out in front watching us about ten yards ahead or twenty yards on the side of this slope and suddenly when the beaters started driving the pheasants an old hare came bounding down the hill and literally went between my two spaniels who were only sitting about a foot apart. This old hare rubbed past these two dogs and they never moved and they were watching me and waiting for me to say "Get him" and of course I didn't because the hare hadn't been shot at. So they just sat and watched him run away and I and everybody just couldn't believe their eyes as they saw just how obedient these two little devils were, watching this old hare come down the hill and run between the two of them. Not many dogs would have done that, except some very highly trained ones which have been trained for high class field trial work.

That is another subject which I could talk about, because my springer spaniels originated from a breed from Northamptonshire where a dear old friend of mine, Bob Gent, a farmer and naturalist bred spaniels and labradors. He was connected very closely with the real spaniel and labrador breeders and dog handlers, the Chudley Brothers, Jack and Keith. They were famed for their dog handling and training. They could breed spaniels for field trial work and anybody who wanted to train a spaniel or labrador for shooting knew they were the people to go to. Luckily for me I had a strain of spaniel from their breed and I was very very thrilled to realise that my old bitch Sue produced pups which were clever and obedient and easy to train.

Many of my pups I sold to friends of mine in Norfolk and around, and so we have now got a good strain of springers in North Norfolk especially who carry on the traditions of their fore-fathers and fore-mothers. My old Sue was a staunch founder-member of that range of dogs. I used to go up to the field trials in latter years filming the trials of labradors and springers and go to the kennels and also film them and I have had my old friend Jack Chudley on television with me to tell us all about his dog training years and showing us how he trained his dogs.

I think with regard to sporting dogs my friend in Northampton taught me a lot. He is Bob Gent, a farmer friend of mine who I have known for many many years, because he is a keen shooting man as well as a naturalist. He used to love to come down to our part of the coast and do a bit of wildfowling with me in the early days. Then I would go back to his farm for the odd week in the winter months and have a shot at one of his pheasants and enjoy his farm. It is a natural history lesson to anybody because his hedges were so nice and the corners of many of his fields were rounded off and filled in with trees and shrubs to encourage nesting sites for game birds and all the other kinds of little birds who wanted to nest there.

Bob and his many friends came down often to see me.

One in particular, D. J. Watkins Pitchford ("B.B." was his *nom de plume*), stayed on Blakeney Point quite often and stayed with my mother in the early days. He wrote many books on wildfowling and sport and natural history. He always wrote as BB, and he and Bob brought their dogs with them to the Point to do a bit of flighting with me, now and again, after a few duck. In the summer months they would come and enjoy the nesting season on an odd day, but Bob's spaniels intrigued me, and I have said I went on to spaniels, but in Northamptonshire they use a labrador and a spaniel together when they are out shooting. Most of these chaps like to let the spaniel do all the rough work hunting out all the hedges and the labradors go in to retrieve as soon as a bird is shot. Sometimes they would have to hunt a long way after a running bird which was wounded and couldn't fly but could run. These "runners" as we call them are picked up very quickly by long-legged dogs like a labrador with a good nose and so that is how my connection with spaniels and Northamptonshire developed.

As the years went on after the war, we returned to our usual influx of visitors especially regulars. Mr. Novaro came with his old friend "Will Watch" Long who sailed him about and taught him all he knew about sailing and he was his boatman. They sailed down for breakfast very often to the Point, he and one or two other people who came in the pre-war days. They returned back to that routine after the war and Mr. Novaro stayed with my mother on the Point on many occasions. On this particular occasion he came with a lady friend as he said to my mother and she said, "Oh I'll put her up as well if you want me to, but she said she will have the room that you generally sleep in and you'll sleep downstairs in what we call our Bunk Room, on the Point." We never had many bedrooms to spare. The lady enjoyed her week's sailing with Novaro and Will Watch Long and when she departed mother said, "I wish you would sign my visitors' book. I always get everybody to sign it." My mother nearly fell through the floor when this lady signed her name as Lady Anne Bowes-Lyon, much to my mother's delight and how proud she was to show that signature to many other people who came to the Point years after.

Prince Philip, as I have said, often came with Lord Buxton, who was then Aubrey Buxton to everybody, he is AB to me, a short abbreviation. On one occasion Prince Philip dropped in for breakfast with his helicopter and my mother served him with breakfast and I took him and Lord Buxton around the nesting grounds to see how they were progressing.

Prince Philip was a very keen naturalist and enjoyed looking at the various nature reserves on our coastline, as well as being a sporting man with a gun. He is a typical Norfolk Naturalist as I would say, he would respect everything in the right season and this is how it should be done to my mind. I had a great honour on one occasion. Prince Charles used to come down with his father

75

Blakeney Quay in winter.

Blakeney Point in summer.

Their Royal Highnesses the Duke and Duchess of Kent and family with Sir Zoll Zuckerman say "good-bye"

to Cley and Salthouse Marshes in the winter months, they were shooting ducks there at certain times of the year. Lord Buxton had Salthouse Marsh and on this occasion I was asked if I would entertain Prince Charles and his cousin around Blakeney harbour during the afternoon or the day to specifically point out various members of the wildfowl family which could be shot and those that couldn't be shot, protected birds in particular. I had to make sure Prince Charles recognised the birds if possible, so that when he became interested in shooting he would naturally know the species he could shoot on the foreshore and those that he couldn't. This was the whole idea of the operation and I had him out for several hours at a time and a delightful young chap he was to take around. We finished up on this occasion joining his father and Lord Buxton at Salthouse Marsh, and our local police sergeant, one George Chapman who was a great friend of everybody locally was there (he was an ex-Grenadier Guard). Many stories can be told about him because he was such a likeable character. He would join in any kind of sport or activity in the locality.

Sergeant Chapman was on duty keeping an eye on security for the Duke, and in particular his guests and I went down to Salthouse because I was invited. Prince Charles and his cousin were along the bank with their little 28-bores, an unusual gun and quite rare, but they had a 28-bore gun each which they first learnt to shoot. They were down on the edge of the reed-beds to have a crack at a duck. It was the early stages of their experiences of shooting and it was quite a cold old night. Billy Bishop the Warden and gamekeeper of that shoot and Billy Bishop's son, Geoffrey, was told to keep an eye on Prince Charles and his cousin to see if they were all right. Geoffrey was sitting on the bank with the sergeant and me about 800 or 900 yards away from where the prince and his cousin were down the bank. George Chapman said to young Geoffrey, "You had better go and see how they are getting on, that is what you are here for you know." So off went Geoffrey and it was a reasonably still night and suddenly out of the gloom we heard Geoffrey's voice, "Are you all right, Charlie boy?" in broad Norfolk. George Chapman, I thought, was going to drop dead, the shock to think that our future king was being called "Charlie boy" by Geoffrey a little bit older than Prince Charles himself, and so this is another story which was told on many occasions, especially by George Chapman.

6 | Later Days and Earlier Memories

Blakeney Point was jogging along very nicely thank you and one of my best friends from the University College in London who took a Professorship and looked after his students on Blakeney, he was Professor Jane a very likeable man and very clever and sort of a distant pupil of Professor Oliver. He was very very strict about the original routines and policies of Blakeney, and he later became Chairman of the Committee. He and I were great friends and we conversed a lot, planned about various things for the future which have been put into practice eventually.

He liked to get down to the Point in the autumn after the high tides. With a few students he did his own research on various subjects on the Point, and I think he liked a bit of photography as well. It was agreed with me that we could go ashore with the students on their last day on Blakeney after their long sessions. Sometimes we took them up to Blakeney for an evening sociability and Professor Jane came with us and we used to finish up at the White Horse to see Aunt Susie and her husband Charlie Long, Stratton and Walter's father and mother. We used to have a wonderful evening. If the tide was right we could go straight up to the quay on the flood tide at about 7.30 p.m. and come back again about 10 p.m. and just scrape out on the last of the tide.

Scrape was the word we used to come down the channel with a boat full of these students and my assistant up forward and looking out for the beacons in the semi-light or moonlight, but it was nearly always dark and we had to more or less judge the way out. We very often got accused of knocking beacons down. The next morning Stratton would ring me up and pull my leg and say, "Look, you want another set of beacons put up after you lot have been up here, we don't know where the h--l we are."

It was all in good fun and these were pleasant evenings we had with various members of the staff from London University. We would perhaps take the students back the next morning to catch their early morning train, there would be struggles to convey all the students with their bits and pieces of luggage, especially at low tide. They had to lug all their gear down to the ferry at low tide and go across the marshes and catch their respective bus or taxi back to Sheringham station to convey them on the early morning train to London. Very often they finished up in Sheringham with mud up their legs, all over their going-away suits, rather amusing. But I think that they enjoyed their stay. I have had many of them respond to their few days at Blakeney and ring me up and say how much they had enjoyed it and how much they had learnt of that wonderful reserve which offers all kinds of subjects to people who felt inclined to explore them.

Charlie Long, Stratton's father, he was the Lifeboat Coxswain at Blakeney, the last coxswain, and the old lifeboat at Blakeney was housed in our Lifeboat House on the Point. She was moored in the harbour from about 1921, I think, the old Lifeboat House was discarded and given to the National Trust in 1923. The lifeboat was a rowing and sailing boat and I can only just remember one of her exploits, when I was quite young. A sailing barge called the *Fred Everard* came ashore on the East Point. There were two chaps aboard her. She was one of the old Thames barges. The lifeboat from Sheringham, which was a rowing and sailing boat came to help her. Not many lifeboats had engines in those days. She sailed down with a nice north-east gale behind her. The Blakeney boat had to tack out of the harbour and then they had to row the boat up against the wind to join in the standby watch on this barge in case she came to real grief, then they had to try and rescue these two people on the barge.

Eventually she bumped ashore on the length of her anchor rope, the seas receded and she dried out and all was well. The Sheringham boat came back to Blakeney for shelter with the Blakeney lifeboat crew leading them in. I will always remember this. They got in on the last of the tides and left both the lifeboats moored on the mainland side of the harbour near Morston Marshes and of course they all finished up in the Morston Anchor to celebrate their trip. Cold, very very cold, weather it was and after many hours of rowing and sailing you felt like something inside you. They used to finish up in the nearest pub and on this occasion they all had a wonderful time, getting "three parts cut" I think.

The story goes that Jimmy Dumble who was the coxswain of the Sheringham lifeboat, Charlie Long, of course, of Blakeney were really merry and enjoying life and a bus was sent to take the Sheringham crew back to Sheringham. They decided that they would leave their lifeboat there moored in the harbour and pick it up as soon as the weather had improved. They said, "Come on, Jimmy, the bus is waiting for you," and he said, "Oh you clear off I will go on my own b————— bus." That is how I heard the story and in the end I think that they left Jimmy in Blakeney and he was transported back independently later on, in the early hours of the next morning.

They were great friends all these fishermen and lifeboatmen and co-operated on every occasion. Many of these lifeboats when they were taken out of service, like the one at Blakeney, were bought quite cheaply and used for fishing and other activities. During the war the lifeboats were used to evacuate troops from Dunkirk. One in particular from Blakeney, I think, was used for a volunteer crew to go and bring back some of our soldiers. Most of the lifeboats by that time had engines put in them and so they were quite efficient and useful.

As the years went on I found myself getting more involved with the lifeboats and coastguards and we had all kinds of sad casualties. One which I shall never forget involved Professor Oliver's sons, both of them naval characters, one was a Rear Admiral, Geoffrey Oliver, and the other was a Captain Engineer in the navy, Captain Philip Oliver. They were both very nice characters, they loved Blakeney Point and they spent many of their holidays at Blakeney in the old Black Hut in the early days, just after the war. The Rear Admiral and his wife were down with their children and tragically the little girl, and a friend who was with her, were swimming on the other side of the Point in rather a rough sort of tide as far as we could gather. The next thing I knew was that the Olivers came rushing in to me and said, "Come quickly one of our little girls is missing. Patience was swimming out there with her friend and she has disappeared." We rushed out as fast as we could and put things into action. It was a real tragedy – this nice little girl was missing.

Eventually with the help of Major Blount of Cley who was always ready to co-operate with rescue work, we had a Land-Rover at our disposal. He would always come up and along the beach in a hurry with a doctor, or anything to do with rescue work, if we needed it. We just had to give him a signal or ring him up. He and I had our own private arrangements with regards to rescuing so that we could get about the place in a hurry and he had his own private aeroplane. He flew up to search for this little girl the next day and I went out with a sergeant in my motorboat down in the harbour, searching the channels. We had all agreed the time when the plane would come over and search. If they saw anything they would give us a flare and sadly we saw this red flare go up from the aeroplane and we went straight out to the sandbank and landed there and discovered the child, she had been drowned and laid there overnight on the ebb tide. Great was the sadness of everybody. She was buried in Blakeney churchyard.

Other times we had some brighter sides of rescue. We had on one particular night to rescue three or four people from a yacht, and then we had another chap who we didn't even know was in trouble. He was round the corner with his little dinghy and apparently his outboard engine had cut out and he was sensible enough to realise that since he had no anchor but plenty of rope on board that he was drifting out through the bar and that he would get swamped and probably drown if he didn't stop his craft from drifting, so he tied his outboard engine to the end of the rope and threw his engine over the side and this acted as an anchor, and then he sat and waited. This was his own story to us the next morning. He sat and waited and when the tide was a little lower he jumped over the side and swam ashore and crept up to us. He was quite exhausted and we suddenly heard a crash on the door and there laid this fellow wet through and exhausted and he said, "Help me." We took him in and brought him round and did what we could for him and he told us this story. I said to him that he had shown initiative and that it would also teach him a lesson too, and I hope a lot more people, never go round that corner or anywhere near the sea, or out in a dinghy, without taking a good anchor and rope with them. He had had plenty of rope but no anchor and this I hope everybody will take note of in the future.

It is essential that whatever you do with a boat, sailing, or rowing, or motoring that you must have a good anchor and rope so that you can throw it out and lay at anchor and wait for somebody to come and help you. This chap we took back along the beach and went out and got his dinghy the next day. We pulled his poor old outboard out on the end of the rope. I expect that he dried it out and got it going again eventually when he got it home.

There are many occasions when we had to nip round the corner with our little motorboat and pick up silly people who were drifting about, some of them had lost their oars and some of them had turned over their sailing dinghies. Many many times these sort of incidents happened. This was one of our honorary duties on Blakeney Point. You had to teach your assistants who you had for the season to be alert and watch all the fishing-boats in and out of the harbour. We would log them daily so that when the coastguards rang up and said "Have you seen fishing-boat so and so" you could say yes or no, with quite definite knowledge. We took note of all their numbers and descriptions so that they could be recognised quite quickly. Now and again we got rewarded with a few fish if we did one or two good jobs for the fishermen in and out of the harbour, on a foggy night, or give them a signal when the tide was a bit awkward and so we all worked together.

Perhaps the saddest rescue I ever did, and which will stick in my memory as long as I live, was at Easter of all days. We took a few people down from the quay at Morston just for a trip out on Easter morning to have a look at the seals and to have a look round on the Point. Various people we had met staying in the hotels and various places came year after year and said, "Look, take us out for a blow", and out we went. About twenty of us went in my ferry boat. I was going to land them on the beach near the Lifeboat House then I thought, "No, I'll let them out at the end of the Point", so out we went to the

Point and landed on the spit there. As we were jumping out of the boat, somebody said, "Oh look, there is an old seal out there in the sea." I had a quick look and thought d——— that's no seal, it's a chap's head bobbing about, and I said, "Good God, there's a couple of people in a canoe or one chap hanging on to someone, upside down", and I said, "Jump out quickly", and they all jumped out. There were two friends of mine in the boat and I said to them, "Look, two volunteers are needed. We'll go and try to get this chap, we can just about do that with this boat, she'll stand a good bit of sea." Off we went and we got to this chap hanging on to a canoe which was upside down and he just laid on the top unconscious more or less, hanging on as best he could. We dragged him on board, pumped him and tried to bring him round, but he was pretty well gone, frozen stiff, and we rushed him back to the house.

My mother was in the Lifeboat House over that Easter weekend and she quickly got this chap warmed up and changed his clothes and rolled him in blankets and as soon as he came round he started to shout out for his brother Francis, and I said, "Good God there's another one out there." So we rushed but we couldn't find the canoe. It had gone farther down and tragically we found the canoe next day with his brother underneath it, all tangled up in the lines.

It would appear that these two brothers had set off from Brancaster to canoe down to Blakeney, in not very good weather. I can assure you, I wouldn't have even dreamt of it, or advised anybody to do it in such weather, but these were two apparently experienced canoeists. They had done quite a lot of this in Norway. They were, I found out afterwards, Sir Edmund Bacon's nephews, our Lord Lieutenant of Norfolk's brother's boys, and this was a very tragic time. The police were alerted and they met me on the quay. One of the police cars rushed the surviving brother to hospital where he was found to be suffering from exposure, he was ill for about a week and then he was fine.

But, going on about these various rescues, let's talk about one which was highly amusing, just to brighten things up a bit. This particular evening I was watching a yacht coming along from Sheringham, the sea was fairly calm but quite a heavy sea, not much wind but just a little bit of onshore wind and these people suddenly dropped anchor outside the bar. The tide was sort of half in and half out and it was ebbing slowly and I thought, "Well that's a daft thing to do to drop anchor there, at this time of the evening. If they are going to stop there all night they'll find that they will be high and dry by low water and they will be in trouble, because the sea will break over them as the yacht touches the bottom and the tide goes out." So I tried to draw their attention, but no luck, they were down below somewhere and it was fairly dark, so I had a yarn with the Sheringham lifeboat and I said "I don't know, but I think you had better come and pluck these people off this dangerous position, or stand by them." So their secretary launched the lifeboat and down they came.

By the time the lifeboat got there they couldn't get in close enough to her and the occupants on board the yacht they couldn't make hear at all. I had some students with me with a lifeline and all our onshore rescue equipment. I had some fairly tough young students and one of them was nearly six feet tall. I detailed him to be off at the end of the rope and he tied this round his waist, he had a bit of slack as well that he could throw to the yacht if he could get near it. He did try and get within about ten or fifteen feet of the yacht, she was bouncing about and any minute now we thought she would start shipping water from the breakers and eventually a head appeared, out of the cabin top. We saw a young chap and we said, "Come on for God's sake get out of that boat, you're going to lose your life if you are not careful." So he bobbed down below and called his crew out.

Much to our amazement, there were two young ladies with hardly anything on, they had been sleeping off their trip I suppose and this was about 11 o'clock at night and we said, "Look, you'd better jump for it and get ashore." Well without any hesitation they did jump and I suppose much to the delight of my students they had the job of passing these young ladies from one to another until they got ashore, and they only had their pants on as far as we could see. We had a few coats with us, so we wrapped the girls up in the coats and got the chap ashore as well and after we went back to the house to get warmed up and have a cup of tea. We got back to the Lifeboat House and my mother was obviously waiting for something to happen, she was standing by the telephone in case I sent a message in. She opened the door and I said, "Come on, mother, I've got some casualties here, they want warming up and a drop of hot soup or something." We pushed the girls through the door and she took one look at them and said, "You lot keep out of here, they've got nothing on." So typical of my mother, she slammed the door and made us lot wait outside in the cold until she got these girls in some sort of comfort wrapped up by the fire and then we were allowed in the kitchen. This highly amused us, although we weren't amused at the time. Afterwards we always laughed about it and I said, "Whatever would you have done, mother, if you had seen us hauling these girls out of the yacht."

That was a good pleasant experience, not just for me but for all my students. I think that they thoroughly enjoyed that night of fun, as they called it, when we had to rescue these girls and this silly young man, who thought that he knew about yachting and seamanship. By morning we found his yacht on top of a sandbank and we did manage to bring her anchor in and let her float higher up into the bay, so we could tow her to safety on the next tide, which we did. In the meantime the crew, the skipper of the yacht had buzzed off ashore and gone back to their respective homes. We were left to report the yacht to the coastguards, who duly had to sort it out. The rightful owner then came and claimed the yacht, because as far as we could gather it was a hired yacht from some firm or other. They hired yachts out to people like those we had just taken off that night, which was rather silly I think. That is how these people so easily get into trouble, through inexperience at sea.

In 1950 I suddenly got information from Miss Gay, the Secretary of the Norfolk Naturalists Trust that the National Trust was going to manage Blakeney Point themselves from thereon, through an agent. They appointed an agent at Blickling Hall who would then administer the responsibilities that Miss Gay undertook for many years. So he relieved her of her duties and came to meet me, a Mr. Bazille Corbin, and he and I got on fairly well together because he was straightforward enough to admit that he knew nothing about Blakeney Point. He relied on me to help him learn about the place, anything I thought that he should know I would inform him, and we got on reasonably well. He had a Management Committee to consult. Things weren't too well at times with these members of the committee because they had all kinds of rather high and mighty ideas, but thanks to Professor Oliver's original policies, which we adhered to, we got on fairly well.

As I said days went on, years went on. Professor Jane was suddenly appointed chairman and he and I could work the place very comfortably and anything we wanted to sort out we did. He was a very likeable person and he got on well with the fishermen and all the locals, he understood my troubles locally and we gradually improved the old place – we kept up with the times, you had to. More and more people came and more and more ideas were developed.

We were very lucky with our communications at the Point because just after the war when we had several casualties we had no telephone as the coastguards telephone had gone as soon as the war had finished. Luckily I got an enquiry from a person who wanted to bring a yacht into the harbour and he said, "I wonder if you could point me in?" which I have done on many occasions and I said, "Certainly I can see you in if I know when you are coming." So he said, "I'll give you a ring." I said, "You can't give me a ring, because I haven't got a telephone." "What!" he said and luckily for me this particular chap was a telephone manager in Norwich which was our area and he said, "Well we will have to do something about that, if we can." He said, "How about a radio telephone?" I laughed and said, "We'd be lucky, wouldn't we?" and he said, "Yes you can be lucky. I'm allowed to use the odd radio telephone installation in my area. We haven't got one in this area at all, but in Scotland they use a lot across the lochs. The official G.P.O. radio telephone, they run off a battery," he said, "a 12-volt battery." I said, "Well this sounds good to me," and he said, "Well we will look into it", and the next thing I knew, he had written to the National Trust and asked for permission to install this as an emergency telephone for the coastguards and for me. He would put the whole thing in and we would have to pay a rent. It would help if we could get some volunteers to subscribe a little bit to it for the installation.

The next thing we knew we had this marvellous link, to telephone ashore, this radio telephone link as they called it. The only one in East Anglia at the time, which fortunately for me this gentleman had initiated because he had a yacht which he wanted to bring in the harbour. He thought that he could help us out and so he did, in a roundabout way. We helped him out as well, because we made sure we knew when he was coming in. We would meet him at the harbour, which was the safe thing to do, because his yacht was a very deep craft and once you touch the bottom with a deep keel you're in trouble. Of course as time went on radio was improved and I think now they've got an even more up-to-date one, they have even got the self-charging one with a solar panel.

This is very convenient because in later years I could ring up Dr. Acheson, our local doctor, another marvellous character who was a very staunch believer in dog training. He bred a very famous breed of labradors, Bally Duff. Being of Irish descent he loved his black labradors and everybody respected him. He was a great character in the village at Blakeney. There was only one thing he was apprehensive about, when I had to call him out to Blakeney Point he said to me, "For Goodness sake, Ted, get me along the beach, I don't like going across the harbour." He didn't like the water, he was not fond of going across in a boat, a thing that one can't help. My mother was like it, she didn't like going in a boat, if she could help it, but of course she had to.

Anyway I had a special arrangement with Major Blount at Cley Hall, who was on the Committee of the Trust, and past chairman, who as I said before had his Land-Rover. The first emergency we ever had after that agreement, he would ship the doctor along the beach in the Land-Rover and here is another story, about people in trouble. On this occasion we had three or four families bathing together, relations all of them I think, on the outside beach. Apparently a girl got into trouble and a man went out to try and help her and he also got into trouble and the next thing we knew was that they had to be rescued. We got them ashore as best we could, both of them were more or less gone I am afraid but we sent for the doctor and he duly arrived with the Land-Rover transport and I said, "Look, Doc, I think that girl has had it. She's lying there and we have been trying to do what we could for her, but she is dead I'm afraid and the man is just about gone." He got to work on the fellow and eventually he said, "Ted, I'm afraid he's gone as well."

All the relations stood around us on the beach and the doctor got up and said "Ladies and Gentlemen I am terribly sorry to inform you that the worst has happened", and straight away this crowd of people started to rejoice and sing and the doctor looked at them and said, "What the dickens have you got here, Ted?" Those were his actual words because he was so shocked by the response to his announcement. We discovered that they were members of a religious sect and apparently they rejoice when anybody passes on, as far as we could gather anyway. Even at the inquest a few days later these people responded in a similar manner to the announcement by the coroner of his sadness and sympathy to the families concerned, they in turn rejoiced and declared how wonderful it was for these two people to pass-on. We just couldn't understand it and never will do.

With regards to the dogs that the doctor bred, I used to enjoy his company and he would like to go out and pick up pheasants in his spare time with his dogs, at different shoots. He was a good shot at a bird, game birds, and he and I had lots of our own private competitions with spaniels plus labradors and eventually one of his sons started to breed spaniels. I think that the Doc had one for a start and then the son had a nice litter. I took some pictures of them. And so our community was knitted very closely with the natural history and the sporting characters, in whatever profession they were in. We seemed to have similar sorts of pastimes and pleasures. Either shooting, bird watching or sailing. You name it, we were all of a mixed bunch but we were very very co-operative at times.

Sailing was, as I said early on, my love in the early days and still was, and we had our famous regattas at Blakeney for a week in August. Then we had the last race of the season, which I have already mentioned, the Morston Regatta, known to us as the Battle of Morston Creek. It was very very popular with everyone before they returned to their respective businesses and homes after their summer holidays at Blakeney. The Morston Regatta was the last event of the season. They would all turn up and take part in this sailing race of ours, which we organised. Major Hamond was at the finishing post with his 12-bore gun. Until his death he took a great pleasure in taking part in acting judge and standing by at the winning-post. As these craft sailed in, the major's old 12-bore would roar out, with a blank cartridge, and sometimes a live cartridge, so I am told, because you would hear a splattering on the mud about four hundred yards away after the lead shot had dropped out of the sky.

All these memories will remain with me for some time yet. I think of the creek at Morston. If you don't know it, after you have read these accounts you will discover what I mean, because it was so twisting and turning you never had a fair wind all the way. You had to tack somewhere down the creek, whether the wind was north, south, east or west, but this was part of the skill. You had to manoeuvre your craft, to know the tides, to know the depth so you could just drop an inch or two of centre keel down to help you tack. If you had

A Ringed Plover and chick nesting on the Point.

Above:
Glandford water mill (converted), part of Bayfield Hall Estate.

Below:
The old Lifeboat House on the Point at high tide.

too much down, of course, you would just touch the mud and you'd had it. Especially when you are racing.

International dinghies were pretty hot in the wind, Internationals were good. I was very lucky to obtain an old International dinghy, a K37 built by Morgan Giles of Teignmouth on the south coast somewhere. Whereas the famous Uffa Fox 14-foot Internationals were diagonally built, the Morgan Giles I had was carvel built which meant that the planks went from stern to stem, whereas the diagonal were up from the gunnel down to the keel in a diagonal formation. The centre keel was about a hundredweight or a little over, a terrific craft to sail. I had many hours of enjoyment on this fourteen-foot craft which was called *The Water Witch*. *The Water Witch* gave me tremendous pleasure and many others as well who used her and sailed her. I won one or two cups with her, much to my delight. She was a lovely dinghy.

I had some good tuition and many challengers because there was a superb sailor as well and Will Long and Freddie and all the rest of them, there was young Billy Long who I haven't mentioned up to date. He was a character well known indeed in the harbour. Like his father Will Watch Long he was a fisherman and a good dinghy sailor, superb. He liked to sail sixteen-footers as well if he could get a chance from various people that he looked after and sailed for in Blakeney. Apart from his love of sailing and fishing, like many other, he was also a very good footballer. In my young days football was a very keen sport locally, the various villages played one another and there were lots of football teams. Nearly every village had one. Billy was so good he played for Sheringham Town I think, in his early days, and then as time went on of course like all the others Billy aged and just settled down to the odd regatta and sailing about as part of his leisure and his job for other people.

I also had the chance to sail for my old school mate, Ted Grimes, who followed his father's profession as a builder. He also loved boats, and built a lot of dinghies. One in particular he set about to make, to compete with the larger craft in Blakeney Sailing Club, a boat called *The Samphire* which I was quite honoured at the time to sail, and win one or two races for him. We even got as far as Wells, foreign parts in those days, and took part in their regatta. So I found myself, much to my delight, doing all the things I had dreamt about, with regards to following in my father's footsteps and sailing in Blakeney and wildfowling. I actually became Chairman of the Wildfowl Association for a time at Blakeney and I helped them to get a long-standing agreement with the National Trust with regards to the shooting rights for the Wildfowl Club in Blakeney and District.

Major Hamond shouldn't be forgotten. He will never be forgotten in my village, until us old village hands who have lived there all their lives have gone. We still talk about him and one of our best subjects is Major Hamond and the Stiffkey rector, the famous Stiffkey rector. Major Hamond was our church warden of course and treasurer and Morston Village was part of the Stiffkey rector's living. He used to come to Morston every Sunday if possible and hold a service. He used to rush down from London, because as many of you will remember he was notorious and got into serious trouble for trying to "protect" young ladies, so he said, in London. He even brought the odd one or two back to Stiffkey with him at times and although his character was such, he was very much liked by the local parishioners. It was a real leg-pull for me because my mother and father were married in Morston church by the Stiffkey rector, Harold Davidson, and I realised also that I was christened by him in Morston church. I have had my leg pulled many times when I divulged this to my shipmates during the war.

Phil Hamond, he had a wonderful session with the Stiffkey rector. On one occasion this reverend gentleman went up to the major's house and knocked on the door to see the major and at the same time the major's servant was cleaning the windows above. I suppose he started flirting with her; anyway the major came out and saw what he was up to and got hold of his collar and turned him round and kicked him down the steps. For that assault Major Hamond was up before his colleagues, the magistrates at Holt, and he was fined five pounds for assaulting the local vicar. He came back full of the joys of spring, so I was told afterwards by my uncle who was just a couple of years older than me, Kitchener Bean. Kitch worked for the major in his furniture business; he was a joiner and carpenter apprenticed there with the major and that particular day when the major came back from Holt court, he said, "Right, everybody, you'll have five pounds extra in your pay-packets this week to celebrate." So Kitch said, "Oh I hope you'll do it again, sir, so we can get another five quid." This was a huge joke around the village.

Another lovely story which I must relate was about police sergeant George Chapman who I have already mentioned, he was getting very popular. The major rang him up and said, "Sergeant, come you over here, we've had a break-in. My wife and I were out last night and when we got back we found that the place had been broken into." So away went George to see the major on his bicycle. He knocked at the door and the major said, "Oh come you in, sergeant, and come into my study and I will tell you all about it." So George in his own words said "We went into the study" and he said, "I was trying to think how I could try and start the conversation off and we went into the old man's study." "Sit you down", he said and I sat down and I said, "Good God, major, they've made a mess of this place." "They haven't been in here," he said. "This is the one place they never came." George said, "I felt a proper fool", and he always told that story when he was out with his colleagues at a police dinner.

As time went on Kitch Bean, who I have mentioned, decided that he would come and help me on the ferry boats. I hadn't got time to ferry of course. I was the warden and I helped him whenever I could, but we had all these schools to take across, and other parties. Kitch and my two cousins, John and Graham Bean, who eventually left school helped on the ferry boats in the early days. Then John helped Kitch on the ferries and we had our little ferry concern going from Morston Quay eventually.

One day out of the blue Lord Buxton who was a friend of everybody said to me, "Ted, I've got some news for you, I would like your help if possible, come and see me." So I went over to see him and he said you wouldn't believe this but he said, "Lord Townshend and I and one or two others have decided to have a television station in Norwich, an ITV station." I said, "What, you're pulling my leg." "No I'm not," he said, "I think it will be quite interesting and I want you if possible to assist me on a natural history programme, since you have done a lot of filming already and you lecture to various people and I have seen your films. I think that you and I can get together and entertain our viewers from time to time with a natural history film and stories." I said that I would love to have a go as I knew that his story was genuine and he laughed and said, "Right, off we go then."

This was about 1960 I think and from thereon I spent some of my spare time in the winter months filming and he and I appeared in the early days on a programme called the "Midday Show" and it is hard to believe now that I look back on it that he and I could sit at midday and talk about natural history in amongst the other items which were on that show including various well-known singers! This seemed to be quite successful and then we branched out a bit further and we did an evening show, or I did it myself with various guests. It developed into quite a well-known programme.

Then the next bit of excitement with regards to the natural history filming. Aubrey Buxton said, "We are starting a big series up called 'Survival' which will be produced in London with contributions from you and other people who we can persuade to help us. From then on of course the Survival programmes were produced. This was in the black-and-white days before we could transmit in colour and so I helped to make one or two of the first Survival programmes, which I enjoyed very much. This also taught me a lot. From then on I was asked to film various subjects around the country or around Britain.

Eventually after a few years Aubrey Buxton said, "Look, would you like to work for us full-time?" and I said, "No, I don't want to do that, I don't want to leave Blakeney Point, but what I will do, with your help we will arrange with the National Trust that I have the winter off each year and film permanently during the winter months and help you with your programmes in general and let someone do my job at Blakeney in the winter. I will ask my cousin John Bean." This he did eventually and right up to the time when I retired from the Point I spent six months with Anglia Television and six months on Blakeney Point during the summer and this went very well.

I found myself being sent abroad much to my delight. One of the exciting trips to me was that I was asked to accompany a film unit, who were making a feature film on the R.A.F. boys on the Island of Gan in the Maldive Islands. There was an R.A.F. Station there and I was to go out and take odd shots of the wildlife to include in the film. This I had to do on several occasions which was very enjoyable. We found ourselves on Gan for the week to make this film. I had a good chance to search the place because it brought back a lot of memories for me. During the war we used to control those islands looking for Japanese fuel dumps for their submarines. We worked from Colombo controlling all those islands and to land on ones like Gan.

The R.A.F. made up quite a large population. The biggest joke was that there was only one lady on the island from Britain. She was in charge of the welfare side of communication for the R.A.F. boys back home. She was a volunteer lady who helped them with matrimonial troubles if they had any. Anyway I discovered on this island that the R.A.F. had got a two-mile runway there, which they cut from the jungle. This was cleared. Not only aircraft landed but birds of passage could land I realised and they had dozens of different species migrating now using Gan on the stripped areas each side of the runway. There is just a small piece of jungle left in which to my delight I found all sorts of creatures around. The fruit bats were a nuisance because all the accommodation huts of the R.A.F. were sheltered by Indian Cherry Trees, which was a favourite food of fruit bats and of course these great old things used to come out at night and play up merry h——— and keep everybody awake until you got used to them.

One delightful bird which I have seen at a distance many times at sea in the Pacific and the Indian Ocean was the Fairy Tern. I found a pair of them nesting on Gan and I filmed them. Marvellous creatures. I filmed them in the fork of a tree, just one egg and no nest. The egg is stuck to the tree with a sort of substance with which the bird covers the egg when it is laid apparently. Also a little green heron which was another rarity to me. I bumped into this chap on my travels around the island. I put up a hide or two to try and film the various birds that nest in the cactus trees and as fast as I put a hide up the natives pinched the materials to wear. You saw lots of natives running around with parts of my hides wrapped round them for loin-cloths. Nevertheless it was a very pleasant time I had there. One native lad was assigned to me to give me a hand because I went back to Gan for a month to make a Survival film of the birds we found in that part of the world and there again this was very enjoyable. Of course the R.A.F. lads took me out in their craft at off-duty times and we filmed various sharks and porpoises and all the rest of the sealife which we could find. I have many happy memories of Gan.

Then I found myself being asked to go to Holland to make a Survival film on the Polders, the areas near the Zeider Zee which was reclaimed by the Dutch so very cleverly. I was told that I could take one of the film trucks and have a couple of weeks there. I invited my old colleague Bob Chestney to go out with me. Bob and I had a pleasant time though we got snowed in a couple of times. As it was wintertime Bob could get away and join me, and all the geese of the Polders were quite exciting to film, and we got to know various characters out there. We had a very enjoyable time. I went back again in the spring for an odd week before I went back to Blakeney and I found various birds coming back to nest, Avocets by the dozen, Black Tailed Godwits and lots of Harriers. The Dutch had very cleverly planned out their farms and villages and a town called Leystad which had just a few houses when I was there in the early days. It was designed to develop to hold two hundred and fifty thousand people. I think it more or less has this population now.

The Dutch taught us a lot about reclaiming land over here in the early days. As soon as I stepped ashore I went round the Polders and I realised how true this was and how clever these people are at reclaiming and planning new lands with new farms and roads and all the rest of it. I found a few terns nesting on the old Polders and also a Kentish Plover which I was delighted to find with eggs. This was in April just before I went to the Point for the summer. I nipped across with a camera for an odd weekend and took my wife. We went to one or two of the reserves.

Of course another tern which is delightful to see was the Black Tern which nested in Holland. We had a pair nest at Welney Washes a few years later – this is another spot on which we did a programme or two because now the Welney Washes are famed for wildfowl. These wild washes are twenty miles long I think, there is a bank running down each side which again I think the Dutch assisted our forefathers to create.

Here there is a character who I mustn't forget, he got his living like many other people in the Welney area plover catching in the early days. The Green Plover was netted and sold at market and also he went eel catching, I mean Ernie James, a great old friend of mine and I used to go and film with him and stay with him and his wife Doris in a delightful old cottage beside the river at Welney called "Plover Cottage". Ernie and I are still pals to this day and he is very clever at making eel baskets from the willows. He had lots of willows on the edge of the river which he cut at various times of the year to produce his eel baskets. He also made fencing from the willows. Peter Scott knew the area well of course, from his shooting days as well as his conservation days. The Wildfowl Trust which he created obtained part of the washes and a character named Josh Scott, no relation to Sir Peter was the first warden of that reserve where many of the Bewick Swans winter.

Many hundreds come to Britain and they go to Welney. There they are looked after in the sort of typical Peter Scott method of a large area for them to feed and wash and brush up in. In front of the observatories they are fed with barley and wheat and other material which the Wildfowl Trust obtain from farmers locally if possible and in bad weather they are fed regularly every day. You can go and watch them quite comfortably from the very big windows of these observatories. Bird watching in luxury! You don't even get your nose wet because you are all wrapped up in this lovely more or less centrally heated observatory. So today things are quite different.

You can still shoot ducks on other washes of course, the mallard and widgeon, and teal. I think that the widgeon are estimated about twenty thousand strong in the height of the winter. Mallard of course breed everywhere and the swans are a wonderful sight, there are lots of Bewicks and Whoopers feeding on various areas during the day, they are not terribly popular with the farmers of course, they can invade a wheat field in winter and cause a bit of trouble. The washes flood very highly in certain times of the year when the tides are high and there is a lot of rainfall down the New Bedford Cut. There are three rivers there and we made a film around Ernie and his life at Welney. "A Man Between Three Rivers" this film was called. You might get a chance to see it again on television.

As I have said before I have enjoyed many trips abroad on behalf of Anglia Television. I took my wife on one trip to Austria, which we very much enjoyed. It was rather special, we travelled with a crowd of children, then we settled into a small hotel on the edge of Lake Neusiedler on the Hungarian border. This was a wonderful lake where many of the ornithologists gathered who could afford to go to Austria. I found many many birds I had never seen before. The Pendulum Tits that nest there really fascinated me, they suspend their nests from the branches of various vegetation and trees, hence the name Pendulum Tits. There were plenty of Bearded Tits in the reeds of course, but their reeds were enormous. I thought that Norfolk reeds were pretty high and strong but these Austrian reed-beds around the lake dwarfed our Norfolk ones – they were a terrific size. There were all sorts of birds nesting there, lots of Harriers and Great White Heron, Purple Heron and there were many other birds which we enjoyed. Outside our hotel window of all things we discovered what we first thought was a Lesser Spotted Woodpecker, but it wasn't, it was another chap who was in fact a Syrian Woodpecker, very much like our woodpeckers in this country, Lesser and Great Spotted. It was a very tame bird. What did thrill me was to see the Wryneck about there. We see the odd Wryneck coming through on migration at Blakeney Point at various times of the year. (August and September is a good month for them.)

We knew that there were Red Spotted Bluethroats there, an odd one or two but there were more White Spotted Bluethroats. I filmed the White

95

Spotted sitting on the telegraph wires and we discovered the Red Spotted, much to the amazement of the local ornithologists in charge of the reserve, and when we told them where it was they went down this railway track around the lake and found it at the spot where I told them. These chaps had never seen the Red Spotted Bluethroat there before.

The other treat for us was that we went up on to the border of Hungary and Austria. There was very strict security along the border, just like we used to read about, with the pillboxes every so many hundred yards, and a great big fence. Apart from that we discovered the Great Bustards. There are not many of them left these days and there was a small colony. I suppose you would count about twenty or thirty of them marching about this sort of prairie-like area, then they flew up over the border when we disturbed them. Many many other birds including Imperial Eagles which we spotted there as well. Then we went down to a nice little area where there were reed-beds and shallow waters and quite a lot of vegetation, and we found the Spoonbills arriving to nest. We went out there at Eastertime and we were there when the spring birds were coming back to nest for the season. It was a wonderful sight to see all these Spoonbills. Ornithologists in this country, when they see a couple of wild Spoonbills on the coast do a fan dance.

One scaring moment or two for my wife was when we were in one of the towers where the shooters stand and shoot the wild boar. Apparently there are lots of them there and suddenly while I was filming I heard this enormous disturbance in the reeds and fifteen to twenty wild boar came charging down the trackway and my wife luckily was sitting only a few steps up on the tower and they went past her like a train, from nowhere. Had she been down on the trackway I don't know what would have happened. You have to put up with all these bits of excitement when you are filming wildlife, especially abroad.

Scotland was another favourite spot for us and Peter Scott had one of his early reserves up there. The Severn Wildfowl Trust was formed down in the Bristol area, but we went up to Dumfries and there is a nice Wildfowl Trust Reserve near Glencaple on the River Nith. There is a wonderful sight when you get the spring tides, a fortnightly tide coming up in a hurry. What we would call a bore. This sort of tide rushes up the river and creates a wall of water about three or four feet high at first and then it gradually lowers itself down and sweeps up the River Ness towards Dumfries. This was a nice thing to film because it occurred quite often especially on these very very exceptional tides that came in in a hurry.

Of course the wild geese flocks on that side of Scotland are marvellous to watch, there are some wonderful areas for the geese. The Solway Firth is a famous place for the wildfowlers to shoot their Pink Footed Geese and, in the early days, all the other species and many many people who loved wildfowling, and could afford it, went up to the Solway Firth at least once

Left:
A typical shooting day on Kelling Estate.

Below:
Bayfield Hall annual cock shoot with Billy Palmer, head gamekeeper, in charge.

Bottom:
Jack Chudley, well-known gun dog breeder and trainer.

Above:
Blakeney Channel frozen up in 1963.

Left:
The Channel in warmer times. I am "Butt pricking" (fishing for flounders).

Bottom:
High spring tide at the Old Lifeboat House on the Point. Prof. Jane and family keeping the water out. c. 1948.

during the winter months to flight these wild geese. I think that you got just as much enjoyment watching them flying in by the hundred. They would flight out on to the farms and back on to the outer sands during the day. Actually they feed during the day as well, but they used the sands to roost on after they have had a good feed.

We made a Survival film around Peter Scott and his love for the wildfowl and this was made in the Wash in the Sutton Bridge area, because he had this famous old mill down there in which we did a lot of his artistic work. He also had a character who waited on him and took him out flighting, Kenzie Thorpe, who was a marvellous character to talk about. He was a very clever wildfowler come poacher. A book was written by Colin Willock on behalf of Kenzie Thorpe which illustrated very cleverly what this old boy used to do for a living.

Back on Blakeney Point one's memory keeps drifting to and fro. I can't really leave out a little story we called "Timber Galore" and if you have seen the film "Whisky Galore" which was made several years ago now of course "Timber Galore" was a similar story, but on this occasion of course we didn't smuggle anything, the timber came to us on Blakeney Point. A timber ship by the name of *Zore* sank about a mile and a half or two miles off Blakeney Harbour and she spilt all her deck cargo of timber, many thousands of pieces of timber and the first thing we knew was that all our beaches away from Weybourne right down to the sands at Wells and Blakeney Point in particular, was strewed with various timber, in different lengths and sizes. We of course gathered this timber up as hard as we could and made stacks of it, some of it was similar to our four-by-four and some was four-by-two or six-by-three, you name it, all about eighteen feet long and perhaps longer. It was very useful timber, very valuable timber.

The year 1953 was the year of the flood that we had, but this timber came in before that, I can't quite remember the date, anyway the story goes like this. We all collected up the timber and once you had salvage of any sort, including pieces of timber and anything that you can mention that would wash up with any value on the beach, you had to report it to the Receiver of Wrecks at King's Lynn. He was the official receiver for all wreckage and he got in touch with the owners if he could find them and you would get a percentage for salvaging the timber or whatever you had found. The Receiver of Wrecks would make sure you claimed it, this was his job for the Government. We reported I don't know how many pieces, the coastguards had to verify this of course. The local chaps who just got a few dozen pieces would report it to the coastguard as anything over three feet in the timber line in those days had to be reported. If it was less than three feet there weren't really any need to report, as that was classed as sort of dunnage which you could reckon the ship had thrown overboard such as broken-up planks which were good for firewood, but these planks were very very valuable.

We had several hundred pieces at least and the coastguard had to come round and he was directed by the receiver to count your pieces of timber or estimate as accurately as possible, so that he could verify what you told the Receiver of Wrecks in writing as to how many pieces you had got. On this particular occasion he came down to inspect our big heap outside the Lifeboat House which my relations and one or two fishermen had helped me gather together. Farmer friends had lent us tractors and trailers and we collected up all these hundreds of pieces of timber in a nice stack and the coastguard came and scratched his head and said, "Well, Ted, you'd better start counting that end and I'll count this end", and that is what we did. I may have missed one or two pieces, but we counted them up and came to the figure which we told the receiver. One coastguard was not too popular because he was rather a bit too officious at times, he thought he had a wonderful opportunity then to get his own back on some people he used to chase off the beach with illegal gear, and he stood on top of a certain sand dune with a fisherman who had counted his pieces of timber and he said to this fisherman, "Well I know where all the bits and pieces of timber are hid, they think I don't know, but I know what they're up to, they've floated them up the creeks and I have found out all the hiding-places." Of course the fisherman laughed like the dickens in the pub afterwards, he said, "Little did he know that he was standing on about two hundred pieces that I had buried up in that sand dune the night before." And so "Timber Galore" became a repetition of "Whisky Galore".

One nice little story that came out of that, was that an old pensioner at Salthouse, he went and got as much as he could on his bicycle and he was warned by this coastguard, "Now you've got to put that in a place of safety before you can declare it to the receiver." This old chap had a couple of dozen planks, I think, so it was said, and so when the coastguard came around to count these planks, he said, "Where is the timber?" "Over in my shed," he said, "Well you can't get them in there," the coastguard said. "They're too long." "Yes I did," he said, "I sawed them up in three-foot long pieces", and so this old chap had carefully sawn all these pieces up in short lengths which made the timber worth less than it should have been.

The 1953 floods was another story which we can never forget. Especially the people at Cley and Salthouse area, who suffered greatly as did those of Wiveton. The banks burst in many places including Wiveton, and our bank at Morston, but we were very lucky, we never had any casualties. We had a bit of damage done and lots of boats washed up where they shouldn't be on the farms and we had to go and collect them as soon as the storm ceased and the weather brightened and we had finished helping other people to recover the more urgent needs. I was on the Point that particular day when the floods started at three o'clock, I came ashore because the tide should never have been flowing before six o'clock and I came rowing up to Morston Quay on the flood tide just after three and I thought "Good God there's something wrong with the tide books, or this north-west gale is going to bring a real good tide in." And so it did and I was up in my village marking time on the tide and watching the boats at the quay and the moorings with the other chaps and we saw our tide get higher over the marshes and the sea get rougher and one by one we saw our boats being either sunk or washed away.

I rang up the local police when the tide started running over our banks and up on to the road and said, "Look you better warn everybody this is going to be a serious flood tide, it is flooding into our road now and in the lower parts of the village." Nothing was heard of after that message to the police, until about eight o'clock when we had six or seven feet of water everywhere at the lower end of the village, the council houses were flooded and we were completely cut off. We had to go back through the farm to Langham, because each side of our village the roads were flooded. And somebody rang up and said, "Now what's this about a flood, where do you want us to come and put these red lights?" I said, "You don't want a red light you want a few trailer pumps before you're finished." Of course I hung up in disgust.

The next morning I received an urgent message from Sergeant Chapman to come and assist him and would I bring a dinghy on my Land-Rover, if I had got one to spare somewhere. So I brought a little dinghy down and met him at Blakeney and we had to rush off to Wiveton because the water was still locked up right through the valleys there and many many people came to grief, but not quite as many as we might have thought and we had fears of many people getting drowned, many more than actually there were.

One dear old lady who lived in a cottage at the bottom of Wiveton Hill apparently was drowned, so they reckoned. We went down with a dinghy as the tide was receding and I went with Sergeant Chapman and we broke in the window on the top floor, she wasn't upstairs and I went down the stairs and pushed the door open and there was about three feet of water in her sitting-room and there she was drowned in her sitting-room, trying to get upstairs. The tide had rushed in so quickly that this dear old lady tried to get upstairs but the water had shut her door and the pressure was too great for her to open it and of course she just struggled and drowned as the tide came higher.

That was what we reckoned and that was what we more or less knew had happened by the evidence in the cottage. Poor old Salthouse copped it rather badly when the sea came over the beaches there and many houses were knocked about badly. Tales were told for months and of course the *Eastern Daily Press* carried vivid pictures of all the different damage and tragedies that had happened on the coastline. We never had a flood warning, but this came into operation after all these troubles were over. I was never really happy with it and I am amazed today to think that warnings can be so easily transmitted from one to another if there is a surge coming down these coasts.

It is as simple as eating a piece of cake, because if you realise that the tide flows down the coast and people way up in Hull or farther still I expect if it was studied more closely when they start getting floods in Hull, they could warn us six, seven or eight hours beforehand what to expect. Our best position would be if a place like Mablethorpe gave us a warning as their tide ran high. If this system which I would like to suggest was put in operation, there would be nothing to it. The coastguards could pass the word from one colleague to another down the coast and just say, "Look we've got our feet wet, this is three or four feet higher than it should be, you'd better tell the people your way", and that is how it would go on right down the coast. The people at Mablethorpe, when they survived a nasty flood, could ring up Lynn and then Hunstanton, we would get a direct call from Mablethorpe which would give us at least four or five hours' notice to be prepared for such a surge.

Likewise when we copped it, or were catching it badly we could ring up Yarmouth and give them at least four hours' notice and so on right round the coast to the Essex coast. Canvey Island was badly flooded, three o'clock in the morning I think it was, and we were flooded at eight o'clock that night, there was no necessity for those people to suffer any casualties had they been warned when we were flooded to expect an exceptional tide. That is my theory and my practical experience, because since we have had these exceptional tides I have rung up my friend at Felixstowe Ferry who build our ferry boats there (or used to build them for us). I warned him that we had a big tide that night and he said, "Right we'll look out for one tomorrow morning, Ted", and he kept prepared and put extra moorings on his boats, put a few sandbags up round the doors of his workshop and all was well.

Now we get our warnings from the Government Research Station on tides and surges etcetera at Bracknell. We'd had the warning from Bracknell, I was on a flood warning alert with George Chapman our sergeant and both he and I had been called out at midnight to stand by for a high tide. When I looked at my tide book I said to George, "This is one of the lowest tides of the year, what are they on about?" Of course it was perhaps a foot higher than it should have been, but nothing more and so all these warnings tended to make people careless, so when we did get a nasty tide they weren't really prepared for it.

My wife was a Cley girl and she could tell us a lot about the 1953 floods because she was in the middle of it as she was helping to manage the George Hotel at Cley on this occasion. Of course the George got flooded fairly badly, but my wife assisted other people in the village after the crisis was over, they had all the mopping up to do. The people's houses were full of mud and water. Cley was in a sorry state for several weeks afterwards and a lot of things were ruined, and the generosity of various people, the Americans in particular, who were still in the country at the various bases, sent lots of things and sent chaps to help clear up the rubbish and mud in the streets of Cley and Salthouse. Everybody helped one another on those occasions.

Many years ago before the new flood barriers or walls were put up around Cley the parishioners expected to be flooded once or twice a year. The odd six inches or foot of water very often came into the George Hotel, and out again, and this was a recognised hazard at Cley. Now of course things are quite different, they've got this flood protection bank which will hold out for a certain time until it gets exceptionally high and then of course like the 1953 flood things might happen.

Distinguished visitors. H.R.H. the Duke of Edinburgh flew in for breakfast with Lord Buxton.

Rare nesting birds, Black Terns at Welney Wildfowl Trust reserve. The first recorded nesting pair for many years.

Part of the swan population at Welney Wildfowl Trust.

7 | .... And So On, And So On ....

We all survived the 1953 flood. Blakeney Point was knocked about pretty badly, the poor old dunes were bashed about. The valleys recovered quite easily, although the vegetation did suffer. There are different plants in various valleys, for instance Glaux Low is one of the valleys, this is well known at Blakeney by all the botanists and students. It takes its name from a nice little plant, the Sea Milkwort (Glaux Maritima) which was quite rare. There is another plant which lives on the edge of the marshes and certain places on Blakeney, the Sea Heath, known as Frankenia. Many plants on Blakeney survived the flood because they're used to salt water like the tough old suaeda bushes (suaede Fruticosa). "Scrubby Sea Blite" is the common name for that particular type of plant which grows in the shingle banks. It is quite useful and it is used a lot in some places for strengthening the sea walls and banks, with its tough roots and growth that will stand quite a lot of knocking about.

Lots of the dunes on the Point were known by various nicknames, the Long Hills, the Little Beach Way, and one hill which is christened after one Dr. White who has known Blakeney Point for most of his life. He came down with his students from University College. He married a colleague from that college (I think she was anyway), and she used to come down with the students when he was there as well and they did their courting on Blakeney. There is a very nice little hill overlooking the nesting grounds where Dr. White and his wife to be used to sit for many hours and we christened that hill White's Hill and so that is how some of these landmarks were christened, by all kinds of different ways.

We had formations of shingle spits extending down the Point. When the flood came our old far Point was sliced in two and this had to be repaired. It was mechanically repaired, which I was rather surprised about, with bulldozers. They just pushed this gap together again and repaired this breach in the ridge and then as years went on we had this outer ridge forming. This is a natural formation and this is how the Point extended over the hundreds of years. We have got one far Point and we christened the other the New Point, a very good ground for the nesting birds.

They loved this new ridge. The Little Terns in particular and the Common Terns soon realised that this was a new nesting ground. I encouraged the marram grasses to grow by putting a ridge of straw bales across, to catch the sand which powders up at low tide and with a strong northerly wind, onshore wind or even offshore wind sand streams across the ridges about a foot deep and you can trap this sand by putting these lines of bales of straw, not too many of them, this will create eventually a sand dune. Of course once you've got a ridge of sand around the marram, seeds can grow, marram seeds are blown as well, you can plant a few odd bits of marram which help it but couch grass is the best thing to start a sand dune, the ordinary foul grass as we call it on the mainland, if you can get that to grow that will soon spread and make a foundation for the marram grass to form a real sand dune. This I did on the New Point, which you can see today. There are two brand new dunes, about ten years old I suppose.

Of course the marsh in between the ridges is Salicornia Marsh, which is another name for samphire. Our rabbits like to chew and feed on this marsh because there is a lot of grass as well, and these marshes were also a great attraction to the duck, because of the samphire seed. It's an annual plant of course, and it sheds its seeds in the autumn and these little teal, our small duck, they love the samphire seeds as do widgeon in bad weather. There is another very special weed which grows in that marsh called Pelvetia which is a nice mobile weed which grows in the pools. It is very profuse in that marsh and these little mud pools are about two or three inches deep. In my younger days I used to collect a lot of this and send sackfuls to the university, for one particular Professor, Professor Oldham, I think his name was, and he produced Iodine from this and this was a Government-sponsored operation because they made lots and lots of Iodine from this particular marsh, in cases of emergency so I was told afterwards. Blakeney Point produced some products which we never knew about until we lived there.

Of course certain times of the year when we were on the Point in the middle of August the mackerel came in if we were lucky and we could go and get a nice feed for breakfast. Whitebait came by the ton, because the whitebait were driven ashore by these old mackerel; they came up automatically with the tide into the harbour and got trapped and a character who I have mentioned before, a great old friend of mine, Stanley Webster (he was known as the whitebait fisherman) caught, I wouldn't like to say how many tons of whitebait in his lifetime and sand eels too, together with his son. He would very often drop us in a feed, sometimes a mullet because he was a great hand at catching these grey mullet, he had some good nets for the job,

108

Above:
Deer and wildfowl in Holkham Park.

Below:
Brent Geese wintering on Holkham Marsh as indeed they do all along the Norfolk coast.

Sue and Teazle after making short work of a stoat and its young. Their handiwork can be seen on the left.

Above left:
A Common Tern chick attempting to eat a young sand eel.

Above:
Sir Peter Scott and myself. (Anglia TV photo.)

Left:
Time to relax in my boat.

but what intrigued me was the way the terns used to hang around him. They would watch him fishing for whitebait and when they had a lot of chicks to feed, of course if you could get some food quickly so much the better for your family and Stanley used to throw handfuls of whitebait up in the air for these birds to catch and they would rush back to the terneries and feed their respective chicks. There were one or two in particular he could hold a sand eel up to and these birds would come down and take them out of his fingers. We was so intrigued with the terns because as he said sometimes they told him where the fish were and they were quite useful to have as friends.

Stanley was a good watch-dog for me because if he saw anybody he thought was after eggs he would always give me the wink, a signal from his old boat and I was up the Lookout and somebody was up to something on the nesting grounds, or even when I was ashore and he thought things weren't right he would quickly have a look and tell me all about it the next day. So it was tit for tat on Blakeney lots of the time – you tried to help them and they helped you. This was what Professor Oliver used to drum into my head when I was younger and how true it is. How it pays off, to know the various characters and be on good terms. You couldn't help it actually because they were so friendly and helpful and we exchanged all kinds of information on various points. Many of the fishermen would tell me when they saw the first tern at sea, when they were out fishing. The Wells whelk fishermen fished out as far as fifteen or twenty miles very often and they would often pass the word along the coast by bush telegraph that they had seen a tern in the early end of March. This told us that these terns were on their way back for the spring, passing up the coast at sea. Where lots of birds migrate either autumn or spring, fishing-boats take note of these various birds.

I spent some time on a lighthouse on one occasion checking the different birds that came through on migration. They would get attracted to the light and they would roost on the lightships taking a few hours' rest very often. All these little land birds as we call them, the robin, skylarks and various warblers which migrate (it may surprise you to know that the skylarks and robins migrate a lot). The lighthouse keepers are very keen about this, and the lightships I should say as well, the lightships in particular. There is always a lot of information gained from them. One lightship which I know of, *Lynn Well*, once recorded with a strong southerly gale off the land, a hen pheasant crashed on to the decks and they reckon that she was disturbed by a shooting party on the mainland. She flew up high and before she knew what had happened, she flew out and lost her way, saw the lightship, flew down and crashed on to the deck to regain strength. Undoubtedly she finished up in the pot, it would be unlikely that she ever flew off there again, she wouldn't be in any condition to do so. But there it is, that is one record which I had never heard of before and talking about birds we could go on to the subject of bird watching in earnest.

September of course was a great month for migration and all these bird watchers would stay at Cley and Blakeney. Many many bird watchers stayed at the George Hotel at Cley and I was in close contact with some of them. If we had a rarity in the bushes in the morning, when I looked out first thing, I would ring up the George Hotel and tell them what we had got on Blakeney so that they could come and have a look if they wanted to. These were the early "twitchers" if you like to call them such, and they would come along the beach and look for the odd bird.

On one occasion I got sadly wrong with the landlady of the George Hotel. She was a great sport and she liked me to ring up her guests and tell them of the birds that were about, but on this occasion I put my foot right in it. I rang up at lunch-time and said, "Oh, Mrs. Burdett, there's a nice bluethroat just come in the bushes and I don't know whether your guests have seen one this year, but if they want to see one they can come along and see it any time now because he will probably be there for an hour or two." Of course, unwittingly, she went into the dining-room when the soup was just being served and she said, "Oh, Ted has just rung up, there's a bluethroat on the Point." Without more ado the dining-room was evacuated immediately, everybody deserted the George and came down to Blakeney Point. My name wasn't worth mentioning in the George by the landlady or my wife, because they were both preparing lunch and I upset the applecart, or should I say the landlady did because she didn't realise what a bluethroat was. If she had done she would never have mentioned it until lunch was finished.

A boyhood friend of mine who came to the Point and stayed many times with my parents was Michael Cant who got very keen on bird watching. I don't think he would like me to call him a twitcher because he reckons he's a bit saner than that, using his own words, but he was a very keen bird ringer in the early days, just after the war and he used to mist net the rarities, put these light nets up and these birds would go in and he would put a ring on them and release them. This he did with special permission from the Trust because he was a qualified ringer and he had to have a licence to ring these birds in that way and he did lots of ringing on Blakeney with me in the autumn and spring when lots of Wrynecks very often came through and other birds that he wanted to record and ring. I used to ring a little, not too much.

I used to ring all my Common Tern chicks at one time and Sandwich Tern chicks, many of them recovered from West Africa, from Ghana and other places, perhaps a couple of years old or less. The best record which I was very pleased about was a Curlew, which was rung in Stockholm as a young bird, a nestling, we found out about him when we sent the ring to headquarters. This ring was very dilapidated; it was a Curlew that was shot in the harbour and the wildfowler gave me the leg with the ring on it and it was so badly worn that I carefully took it off and sent it to London and they got the information from Norway and this bird proved to be thirty-two years old. This was the oldest recorded recovering of that species known to my knowledge and their knowledge.

My wife-to-be came over and helped my mother quite a lot on the Point in the catering situation, and eventually we were married and my mother retired back to the village. She worked full-time there more or less as an office girl and we had all sorts of excitements up to the time that I retired. My wife, like my mother, had the pleasure of giving a meal to the Royal Party one morning. Lord Buxton brought Prince Philip and Princess Alexandra and her husband and one or two more and we took them out to see the seals and have a look round in general. It was not very nice weather but they enjoyed it and then they all had a meal in the Lifeboat House which my wife provided, much to her pleasure. We were delighted with Princess Alexandra, my wife thought she was marvellous, and we all do, but in particular my wife adored her because of her casual way and friendliness to everybody.

As time went on Lord Buxton's family grew up, we met one of his daughters in particular. She got very keen on wildlife photography and I had the pleasant job of having her with me for two or three months to teach her all the fundamental sides of filming, the equipment to use and how to handle it. We did quite a bit in the locality and I taught her how to use the camera, mainly how to approach birds and anything I could think of like which would make her a reasonable camera woman. She was so keen on listening to my instructions that after I had told her many times that a camera comes first when you are out filming, if you can keep your camera dry it is half the battle.

On this occasion she was down on Billy Bishop's marsh, as we call it at Cley and she was going across one of Billy's perilous planks of wood across a drain and she slipped in, up to her shoulders in water more or less, but she held her camera high above her head and kept it dry and I was rather proud of her over that. She did exactly what we all try to do. So Cindy became known as a wildlife photographer on the Survival series. She went out to the Falkland Islands, before the troubles started actually. She made some nice film out there and then she got clobbered with the troubles and she had to be rescued, and brought back to a place of safety. Nevertheless she continues to produce some good stuff which I am very pleased about, because I am no longer fit enough to film.

Having retired in 1980, I suddenly found myself in Cromer Hospital with a coronary which was not too pleasant, but thank God for Cromer Hospital I can sit here and dictate this story of my experiences in quite pleasant surroundings. I think that these hospitals locally are a credit to Norfolk and I have great faith in them.

In the early days my father was coastguard at Cromer for a short time and I was not very old when I went there, but prior to his retirement from the coastguard service he was stationed at Cromer and then back to Morston where he retired, but for a short space of time he and my mother were housekeeper and chauffeur to Bishop O'Rourke at Blakeney Church, at the new Rectory. I can remember that well because I was at Blakeney School and we were in the choir because our headmaster was the organist and choirmaster. When I tell people and look back at Blakeney and see that lovely church from Blakeney Point, I'd say, "You'll never believe this but I was Server Boy in that church." Sometimes three times on a Sunday because Bishop O'Rourke was very high church and all of us lads were roped in to choir and Serving the Holy Communion. Lots of people think that I am pulling their legs when I tell them that, but it is quite true.

So we come to the end of my experiences on Blakeney. There may be one or two other things that I can think of, which will probably be written at a later date. There are many friends that I would like to mention and talk about and thank for their help during my experiences. Especially Colin Willock, who was the mainstay of the Survival programme, he and I were on good terms and always have been. Colin Willock and I as I have said became very attached to one another through Anglia Television and he was a rare sporting man with regards to wildfowling and pheasant shooting. He had a wonderful gift of remembering every word you said to him in any sort of conversation, a very photogenic memory, I suppose you could say. He wrote many books and articles from actual conversations with various people and so Colin was gifted for the job of editing and script-writing for Survival.

Another character who I cannot leave out of my memoirs, an old friend of mine through Anglia Television was Ron Downing, my film director and programme director. Very often he taught me a heck of a lot about filming techniques for television work and he and I exchanged our experiences. I introduced him more or less to shooting and wildfowling and bird watching and things in general in our part of the world. Ron had come from a busy area before he had joined Anglia Television. He was I think mixed up with the hustle and bustle of London and various places and he appreciated the countryside very quickly and he and I had many hours and days together, sometimes relaxing with a gun and sometimes out with cameras.

There are many good friends in Anglia who I would like to mention but they are so numerous that this would mean another few pages to this book, but nevertheless I am grateful to all of them, all their friendship and help since I joined Anglia to the time I retired. Various editors I had and various other characters who assisted me at various times.

I thought to conclude my book, or memoirs, I would put in the last report I made as warden for Blakeney Point, the last report to the Committee of that

1979 season. This not only was my last report, but a very pleasing one because as you will see when you read it that we achieved the ultimate goal of creating a nature reserve with public access to it.

As Professor Oliver predicted, when we finished in 1979 we had the largest population of nesting terns in the country, in the British Islands. To me this is very very satisfying. Why it could not be published as a report for the general public to see, read, and learn about these nature reserves, I will never know. This, my last report to the Management Committee, is in this book. I thought that this would also interest many people, not just ornithologists, but the average visitor who comes to Blakeney. He likes to know what really goes on with regards the breeding birds and the other reports that have to be researched and reported on. The numbers of nesting birds in this report I am sure will interest many people.

I hope that this book gives satisfaction to many people and encourages them to support reserves such as Blakeney. I don't think that I would have stayed as long as I did at Blakeney had it not been for the staunch support of my right-hand, my wife who was always at hand to help me in every way. To her I dedicate my memoirs and hope that we can enjoy many years together in our retirement.

BLAKENEY POINT REPORT 1979 SEASON

1978/9 winter and indeed the Spring is something to record as regards Blakeney's
survival, of its habitat and its wildlife in particular.

As the winter lingered on, snow and ice came and went reluctantly, in fact, on
the 6th May we had a Ringed plover's nest with 2 eggs with a covering of snow
around the nest. Although I have seen this before, never have we had such
severe cold so late in the Spring.

During the freeze-up, many birds suffered and many birds cashed in on the weak
and helpless wading birds in the estuary. As regards the birds that cashed in,
namely, the harriers, kestrels and similar birds of prey, they could pick off
many small waders at ease, since these creatures were starving and exposed.
So good were the pickings in and around the estuary that we had no less than
five hen harriers for several weeks.

When we returned to the Point to take up residence, the evidence of these birds
could be seen everywhere, in the form of dead frames and wings of Ringed plover's
Redshank, Knot and Dunlin and many other species of both waders and land birds.
Hence the short numbers of Ringed plover's and Redshank nesting population.

Large gulls and a few Herons took an equal toll of these unfortunate creatures,
and so we realised the method of selection by Nature.

The Tern arrived a little late but the most disturbing discovery was the casualties
amongst the Lesser Tern; as they arrived and inspected their nesting sites in this
very severe Spring, many of them just died sitting on the foreshore through
exposure and probably too weak to fish. I found no less than eighteen of these
adult birds. By the 9th May, about 100 Sandwich Tern were sitting on their
1978 nesting site, opposite the Observatory. Also, to note the date, a skein
of Brent Geese could still be seen in the harbour.

Sandwich Terns increased on the nesting site to about 1200 pairs, incubating well
by the 26th May, my first inspection of the site, with Lord Buxton. A few days
later another large congregation of Sandwich Tern arrived and took up residence
on the new dunes at the end of New Point, some 1500 pairs estimated, and after
they had obviously laid, several hundred more settled on another dune 100 yards
away, and so we had the largest number of Sandwich Terns ever recorded nesting at
Blakeney. All we had to do was to encourage the public to help us protect them
from disturbance.

Common Terns were very late indeed to get under way with their nesting season.
The first week in June, when they normally start hatching, was the actual date
when the main numbers had really nested. On the old Point we had about 200
pairs, plus 7 Little Terns by the 4th June and on the outer ridge a nice colony
of Little Tern had established themselves and the whole length of the New
Point was a mass of Nesting Terns, the Sandwich Tern of course making things
very spectacular, as the Committee will confirm, as I conducted them through
that area during their visit.

Having started late, which is always the most successful, weather permitting, because of the food factor, when these chicks of the terns do eventually hatch their natural food by this time should have arrived in large numbers, i.e., whitebait in particular and sand eel. There was, in fact, an explosion of young sand eels in the sea according to the whitebait fisherman, Stanley Webster. Since we had reasonable weather and no high tides, the first attempts were successful and the season finished on time, making it possible for us to take down most of our fencing and allow the public to use the foreshore for their natural enjoyment by mid-August. Apart from large numbers of chicks of the Sandwich Tern still parading about, the only danger was dogs off leads. And so, by mid-August, most of the colony were on the move with their chicks flying. This was obviously a record of success.

Vermin

During the nesting season we had little trouble with predators. Black-headed gulls did try it on and took a few eggs and cnicks, Black-backed gulls snitched a few but we noticed that they enjoyed pinching the Black-headed gull chicks, who wandered about individually into the Black-back's territory.

A short-eared owl did take a few Sandwich Tern chicks and also several adult birds of both species, Sandwich and Common. The usual old thing, in the early stages of incubation, the owls kill these birds on the nest.

Two stoats and one old rat were trapped in and around the terneries, not too much damage, as the stoats had many young rabbits to enjoy.

Birds on Passage

During May and June a few flocks of waders pass through, Bar-tailed Godwits, large numbers of Knot and also for a short time, from the 26th May to the 30th, one Kentish Plover stayed with us, but he was badly treated by the Ringed plover's who objected to him encroaching their nesting sites.

Eider Duck were seen for many weeks, 28th May onwards. Three birds in particular, two duck and one drake in breeding condition were in and out of the nesting grounds on many occasions. We hope this is a sign of future nesters.

A very slow migration apart from early Redwings, late August, early September, a few rare ones, 8th and 12th September, Barred Warblers, Black Redstarts, one Redbreasted Flycatcher and I saw one very poor looking Bluethroat. Brent Geese arrived suddenly in good numbers. The first week in October several hundred could be seen feeding on the harbour edge.

Visitors

Well below last year's figures. Ferries both from Blakeney and Morston were down up to August, although as I write the Blakeney ferries have been averaging 40 a day through October, a very late fine holiday period, mainly bird watchers. Many more walked from Cley or one way, owing, I think, to the ferry costs.

Visitors by ferries	12,000 up to 25th October, approx.
Walked from Cley	3,500
Schools, Students, etc.	3,000
	18,500 estimated

Incidents

The "Concord" tragedy marred the whole Season, as regards the boating fraternity.
I gave Mr. Maurice a copy of my Report of the whole incident for the record.

Sunday, 15th July, one person missing in a dinghy caused a call-out from coastguards and helicopters, etc. False alarm, owing to poor co-operation from
coastguards.

21st July - fishing-boat "Morning Flight" - the skipper contacted me by radio
to call helicopter to lift a passenger off, who was suffering from severe heart
attack. This operation was carried out after a lot of unnecessary delay by
coastguards. This had to be done by helicopter, as the tide was too low to
enter harbour. The casualty was flown straight to Norwich Hospital, where he
was only just saved from his trouble. He is now completely recovered.

Many other minor incidents were reported and dealt with, these I think are
becoming a daily routine and would take too long to relate individually.

In conclusion

I am very satisfied indeed with the past successful Season. The most satisfying
and climax to my years of Wardening on Blakeney Point. To quote an expression
"It is nice to discover" that Blakeney Point in 1978 had the largest colony of
nesting birds in Britain and I reckon that 1979 will be likewise. I wonder
why this cannot be publicised. For one or two reasons, firstly, Blakeney is a
unique reserve, used by all and sundry and it must be seen, if not publicised,
that all credit to the success of the natural history side must go to the
public relationship and co-operation and visitor participation of everyone who
enjoys Blakeney, not the least, the local inhabitants.

I am delighted that my philosophy and policies, taught me by Professor Oliver,
is paying off, whereby, as a boy, he would tell me, and rightly predict that
not fifty people would visit the terneries, but thousands, and he also
stressed that I must encourage people to participate in the protection of this
very special piece of land.

I know that the National Trust and its managing bodies disagree and have disagreed
very strongly, in fact, I have been accused of commercialisation and it has been
written that there would not be a tern left on Blakeney Point in a few years.
This was scribed way back in 1950. However, we must continue modifying control
procedures and interest the new generation to learn and study whatever subject
they are interested in and behave as a Blakeney visitor, whether ski-ing,
sailing or just sleeping the day away, all must have his own routine.

Before I close, my grateful thanks to my staunch assistant, Mr Chris Parker,
for his invaluable support.

BLAKENEY POINT REPORT 1979 SEASON - NESTING FIGURES APPROXIMATELY

SPECIES	NESTING NUMBERS	REMARKS	HATCHING SUCCESS
Sandwich terns	3500 to 3800	Very good	Approx. 2000 flying.
Common tern	800 to 850	Good	500
Lesser tern	160 to 180	Very good	160 chicks flying approx.
Arctic tern	3 nests	Fair	3 chicks seen flying
Oyster catchers	160	Good	numbers flying
Ringed plover	110 pair	Good hatches	Very good broods seen
Redshank	9 nests known		Good hatches
Shelduck	Est. 30 nests	Very good broods	
French partridges	3 nests found	3 small conveys seen	5,4,7
Black-headed gulls	Several hundred laid but destroyed as many as possible. Still about 100 chicks survived.		
Common gull	1 pair		2 chicks
Lesser black-backed gull	2 nests	Only 1 nest hatched	2 chicks
Dunock	3 nests found	Very good	
Linnets	40 nests est.	Good	
Skylarks	30/40 est.	Fair	
Meadow pipits	25 nests		Good
Swallows	1 pair		4 chicks

Ted Eales

1979.

1ST NOV.

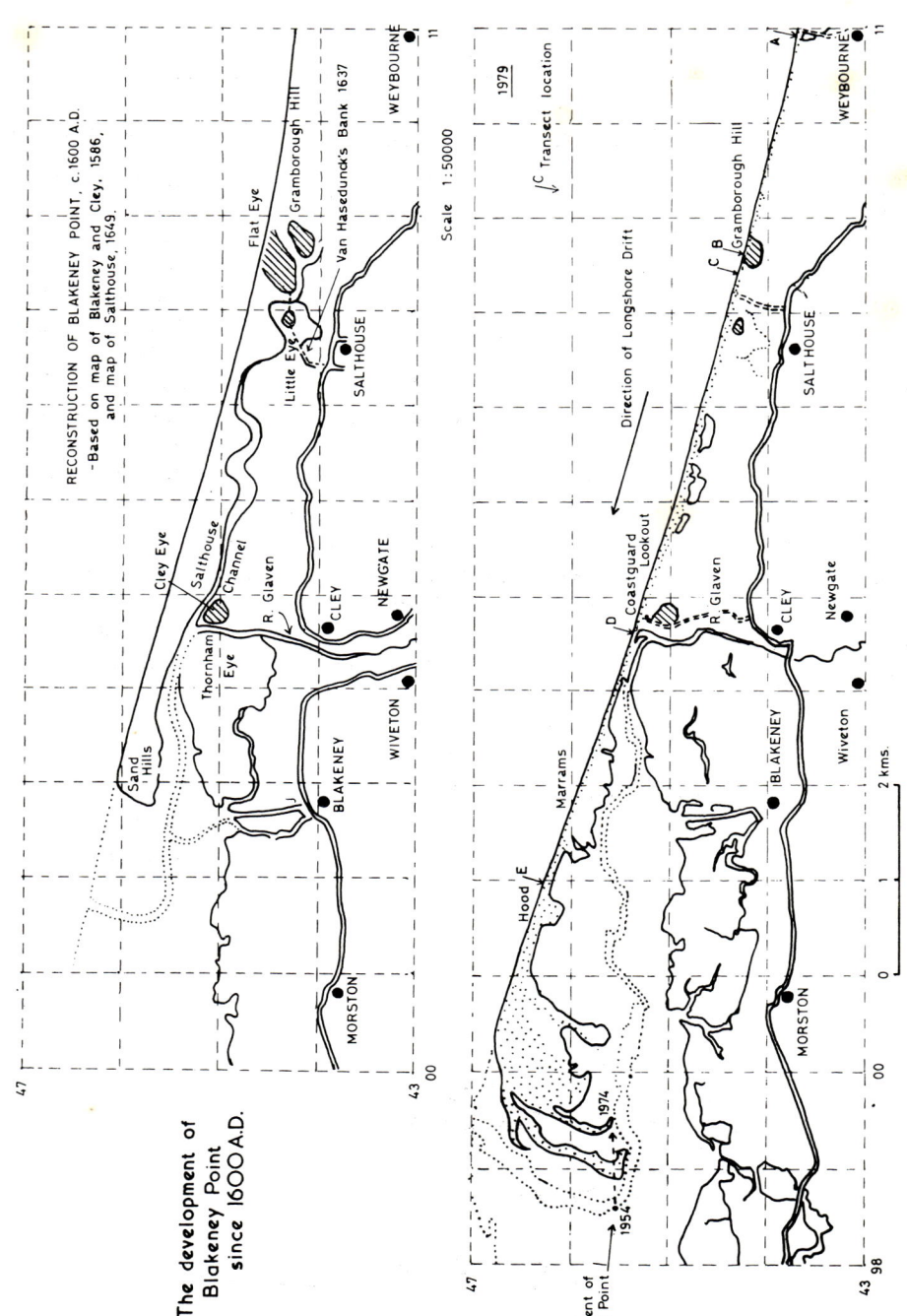

The development of
Blakeney Point
since 1600 A.D.

RECONSTRUCTION OF BLAKENEY POINT, c.1600 A.D.
-Based on map of Blakeney and Cley, 1586,
and map of Salthouse, 1649.

Scale 1:50000

Sand Hills

Cley Eye

Salthouse Channel

Thornham Eye

R. Glaven

Flat Eye

Gramborough Hill

Little Eye

Van Hasedunck's Bank 1637

SALTHOUSE

CLEY

NEWGATE

BLAKENEY

WIVETON

MORSTON

WEYBOURNE

47

00

43

11

1979

Transect location

Direction of Longshore Drift

Marrams

Hood

Movement of
old Far Point

1974

1954

Coastguard
Lookout

R. Glaven

D

E

C B Gramborough Hill

A

SALTHOUSE

Newgate

BLAKENEY

Wiveton

MORSTON

CLEY

WEYBOURNE

0   1   2 kms.

47

98

00

43

11

The probable development of Blakeney Point, shown by comparisons between early maps and a survey in 1979.